The Problem of

EVIL

AND

Suffering

Revised

The Problem of

EVIL AND Suffering

Revised

Edward P. Myers, Ph.D.

HOWARD
PUBLISHING CO.

3117 North 7th
West Monroe, Louisiana 71291

The purpose of Howard Publishing is threefold:

- **Inspiring** holiness in the lives of believers,

- **Instilling** hope in the hearts of struggling people everywhere,

- **Instructing** believers toward a deeper faith in Jesus Christ,

Because he's coming again.

The Problem of Evil and Suffering
© 1978 by Howard Publishing
All rights reserved.
Revised © 1992

Published by Howard Publishing Co., Inc.
3117 North 7th Street, West Monroe, LA 71291-2227

Printed in the United States of America

Cover Design by Steve Diggs and Friends

ISBN# 1-878990-07-1

Scripture quotations not otherwise marked are from the New International Version.

Dedication
to
Mrs. Christine Myers

My mother, whose spiritual influence has always been present in my life. She helped me through many struggles and caused me to believe that when suffering is finished, there is always a better day. Thanks Mom for all you have meant and still mean to me and our family.

Contents

About the Author

Edward P. Myers is now serving as Professor of Bible and Christian Doctrine at Harding University in Searcy, Arkansas. He has served as minister for churches of Christ in Texas, Oklahoma, Louisiana, Ohio, West Virginia, and Tennessee. He attended the Sunset School of Preaching (Certificate), Lubbock Christian University (B.A.), Cincinnati Bible Seminary (M.A.), Harding University Graduate School of Religion (M.A.R.), Alabama Christian School of Religion (M.T.S.,M.Th.), Luther Rice Seminary (D.Min.), and Drew University (M.Phil., Ph.D.). He is a member of the Evangelical Theological Society, Evangelical Philosophical Society, and the Society of Biblical Literature. He has served as an Instructor in Bible at White's Ferry Road School of Biblical Studies, West Monroe, Louisiana; Professor of Bible and Christian Apologetics and Chairman of the Department of Bible and Religion at Ohio Valley College, Parkersburg, West Virginia; Dean of Academics, Alabama Christian School of Religion, Montgomery, Alabama; and as Adjunct-Professor for the Magnolia Bible College, Kosciusko, Mississippi.

Other books by this writer include *A Study of Angels, Doctrine of the Godhead* (co-authored), *Biblical Interpretation* (co-editor), and *Letters to the Seven Churches of Asia.* He is presently writing a commentary for *I & II Timothy and Titus, The Book of Revelation,* and a full length study of *Systematic Theology.*

Acknowledgments

When an author begins to acknowledge his debt to others, his responsibility quickly falls into the realm of "the impossible." To name those to whom I am indebted would be no small undertaking. Having suffered the loss of my father as a boy, I began my questions about pain and suffering early in life. There have been many people throughout my life who have contributed to the shaping and molding of my values. There is no way I could list all whose lives have touched mine and who have played an important part in helping me understand God's direction for a joyous life. The most important is the woman to whom I have chosen to dedicate this work—my mother.

This material was first written for a graduate thesis and presented to the faculty of the Cincinnati Christian Seminary (Cincinnati, Ohio) in partial fulfillment for a graduate degree in Christian Apologetics. Appreciation is here expressed to Mrs. Ron (Johan) Hartman for the typing of the original manuscript and to the Arlington Church of Christ (Cincinnati, Ohio) for allowing the time necessary for the research and writing of this work, while I was at the same time tending to the necessary details required of a local evangelist.

Dr. Jack Cottrell, of the Cincinnati Christian Seminary, gave guidance in the writing of this work. His help was invaluable in understanding the twofold nature of the problem of evil and suffering. Any asset attributed to this writing is due to his help; any liabilities are my own.

Dr. James D. Bales (Harding College, Searcy, Arkansas) read the manuscript and wrote the foreword to the first edition. In this revised edition, it is reprinted as "Appendix 2." I remain thankful to him for his gracious assistance and for taking time from his busy schedule to offer his help.

Dr. John Mark Hicks, a colleague and friend, has written the foreword to this new edition. He has taken the time to read the entire manuscript in its new format and to make comments that he felt would clarify certain points for the reader. In almost every instance, his suggestions were used. Because of his keen eye and sense of clarity, this edition is much better than it would have been without his help.

I would like to say "thank you" to Tom Eddins, a colleague at Harding University. I asked him for help during the last stages of the preparation of this book, and he was always willing to assist. Though these encounters were brief, I am sure he saved me from several mistakes.

I must add a word of thank you to Philis Boultinghouse and the editorial staff at Howard Publishing. This edition of the book has gone through extensive editorial work to make it read better than before. I am thankful for such help.

I would also like to add a word of appreciation to the elders of the Wooddale Church of Christ in Memphis, Tennessee, with whom I labored for six wonderful years as pulpit minister. It was during that time I began the revision of this material. They graciously allowed the necessary time and secretarial assistance for this to be done. Without their support, both materially and spiritually, this would not have been completed.

Finally, I want to say thank you to my lovely wife, Janice, and daughter, Carolyn. They sacrificed many precious hours that could have been spent with me as husband and father, that I might complete this work.

May our God comfort us, as we in turn comfort others through the trials, tribulations, and sorrows of facing the problem of evil and suffering (2 Corinthians 1:3-11; 2 Corinthians 4:6-5:1).

Proverbs 3:5-6

Edward P. Myers, Ph.D.
Professor of Bible & Christian Doctrine
College of Bible and Religion
Harding University
Searcy, Arkansas 72149

Credits

The following publishing companies and authors have graciously granted permission to use quotations from copyrighted materials.

Abingdon Press, Nashville, Tennessee: from Hubert Black, *Good God! Cry or Credo*, © 1966 by Abingdon Press, Used by Permission.

Baker Book House, Grand Rapids, Michigan: from Batsell B. Baxter, *I Believe Because...*, © 1971. Merrill F. Unger, "Satan," *Baker's Dictionary of Theology*, © 1973.

Bertocci, Peter, from *Introduction to Philosophy of Religion*.

Cambridge University Press, New York: from F. R. Tennant, *Philosophical Theology, II*, 1930.

Charles Scribner's Sons, New York: from George F. Thomas, *Philosophy And Religious Beliefs*, © 1970 George F. Thomas.

College Press, Joplin, Missouri: from C. C. Crawford, *Genesis*, II.

Doubleday and Company, New York: from Austin Farrer, *Love Almighty and Ills Unlimited*, © 1962.

Harper & Row Publishers, Inc., New York: from John Hick, *Evil and the God of Love*, © 1966.

Elton Trueblood, *Philosophy of Religion*, © 1957.

InterVarsity Press, Downers Grove, Illinois: from John W. Wenham, *The Goodness of God*, © 1974 by InterVarsity Press, and used by permission of InterVarsity Press, USA.

Prentice-Hall, Inc., Englewood Cliffs, New Jersey: from John Hick, *Philosophy of Religion*, © 1963.

Random House, Inc., New York, New York: from Donald A. Wells, *God, Man and the Thinker: Philosophies of Religion*, © Random House, Inc., 1962.

Southwestern Journal of Theology, from Milton Ferguson, "The Problem of Evil and Suffering," Vol. XII, April, 1973.

The Macmillan Company, New York: from Antony Flew and Alasdair MacIntyre, editors, *New Essays in Philosophical Theology*, © 1963.

C. S. Lewis, *The Problem of Pain*, © 1948.

Victor Books, Wheaton, Illinois: from Paul Little, *Know Why You Believe*, © 1967.

Warren, Thomas B., *Have Atheists Proved There Is No God?* Printed by Gospel Advocate, Nashville, Tennessee: © 1972 by Thomas B. Warren.

Wm. B. Eerdmans Publishing Company, Grand Rapids, Michigan: from Charles Hodge, *Systematic Theology*, Vol. I, © 1907.

Foreword

by Dr. John Mark Hicks

Suffering is something everyone experiences to one degree or another. It is a common experience of humanity. No one escapes it. Everyone has felt both its physical and emotional pain.

At the same time, many find hope and comfort in their suffering through their faith in a benevolent and almighty God. Others, however, find in their suffering the reason to reject God or the occasion to withdraw from God.

While some accept their suffering by trusting in God and others rebel, everyone asks the simple questions: "Why me? Why now? Why this?" These questions are both intellectual and emotional; academic and practical.

The intellectual question has always been hotly debated in the history of theism, particularly Christian theism. The existence, extent, and nature of suffering is the greatest intellectual challenge Christianity must face. If the God of the Bible exists, why does suffering exist? Why does so much suffering exist? Why do innocent people, even children, suffer? Isn't God able to reduce or extinguish the suffering? Doesn't God want to do something about it?

The difficulty of this problem must not be underestimated. It is the stumbling block over which many potential believers trip. Atheists refuse to take seriously arguments for the existence of God because it is inconceivable that God could permit or sanction the existence of suffering in the world. It is the slippery slope on which many believers slide into unbelief. Faced with the practical problems of suffering and the emotional feelings of anger and isolation, some believers cannot reconcile their suffering with God's love. Suffering is the hard rock of reality which every believer must face both intellectually and practically.

Edward Myers does us a service by providing in this volume a survey of both the problem and the proffered solutions. He states the problem succinctly and clearly and searches through the various options for the best available answers.

His purpose is not to provide practical counseling on how to deal with suffering (though many of his points have practical implications). Rather, he deals with the intellectual doubts that arise about God when we hear about genetic birth defects or the starvation of millions in Africa or the death of a family as the result of a drunk driver. How can the existence of an omnipotent, benevolent God be reconciled with the facts of suffering? Is it rational to believe in the God of the Bible when suffering and evil are so rampant in a world which is supposedly under God's control?

If these questions bother you, if they occasion intellectual and emotional doubts in your heart, then you need to read Ed's book. You will profit from the survey of the problem and its various possible solutions. At once you will learn that the problem and its solution is much more complicated than you probably imagined. Ed's book will not answer all your questions (and it does not attempt to deal with all questions; what book can?), but it will provide guidelines for your thinking that are important and, I believe, headed in the right direction. I commend it as your first step in thinking through the intellectual problems that surround "the problem of evil and suffering."

Dr. John Mark Hicks
Associate Professor of Christian Doctrine
Harding University Graduate School of Religion
Memphis, Tennessee

Introduction

One of the greatest challenges to Christianity today, if not *the* greatest, comes not from the atheist or agnostic; rather it comes from the man on the street who tries to reconcile the existence of a powerful and loving God with the existence of evil and suffering. Philosophers and theologians alike often speak and write about this incongruity under the heading *theodicy*. Theodicy comes from two Greek words; *theos* (which means God) and *diake* (which means righteousness); thus, theodicy refers to reconciling the belief in a powerful and loving God with the fact of evil and suffering. In other words, is it possible to (1) recognize that evil and suffering exist in our world and (2) believe in a God who is loving and powerful? Some say no and believe that the existence of evil and suffering in our world is sufficient cause to say God does not exist.

Bernard Ramm has written,

> Theodicy deals with the world we have. What the Christian heart wants to hear, and what the questioning non-christian wants to know,

is what the Christian faith has to say that is
meaningful or helpful with the actual evil and
sin in the world which, in Christian teaching,
is the creation of God.[1]

Robert King writes,

The primary charge brought against religion,
and particularly the Christian religion, in the
modern period has been its failure to deal adequately with the problem of evil. Innocent
suffering both as a result of natural calamity
and human malevolence is presumed to count
decisively against the existence of a benevolent and omnipotent God. A "God of love" such
as Christians profess to worship, surely would
not permit such wanton destruction of human
life as represented by the Lisbon earthquake
or the Holocaust.[2]

The quest of this study is to reconcile the belief
in an omnipotent (all-powerful) and omnibenevolent (all-loving) God with the problem of evil so
there is no contradiction between the two. A study
of this type must begin by setting forth certain
definitions.

Philosophers and theologians of the "Christian
Tradition" hold various views about God[3] that are
in conflict with what the Bible teaches. In this

---

1. Ramm, *The God Who Makes a Difference*, p. 129-30.

2. King, in a review of Diogenes Allen's *The Traces of God*, in
Princeton Seminary Bulletin, III/3 NS 1982, p. 336.

3. For a discussion of various views about God see Trueblood,
Philosophy of Religion, pp. 259-74.

study the word *God* is used to mean "the infinite, eternal, uncreated personal reality, who has created all that exists other than himself, and who has revealed himself to his human creatures as holy and loving."[4] Or, as another has stated, "We are driven to the conclusion that God is the Personal Reality, in short, the Transcendent Person."[5]

God is personal. He thinks, loves, hates, acts, and hears and responds to prayers. God is immanent to the world and yet he transcends the world. God is not the universe, but the One who made it, and he is concerned about what happens to it. Such expressions as these can properly be called "Biblical Theism." Biblical Theism is a belief in a God who is different from the deities of the philosophies and ideologies of men. He is real, personal, and immanent. Any definition that does not include these characteristics cannot be adequately referred to as either biblical or Christian.

God, as defined here, is not to be viewed in a naturalistic way as is done in Finitism. The Finitist believes in a God, even a personal God. But to the Finitist, God is limited in what he can do. His powers, his goodness, and his knowledge are all limited. In essence, God is finite. A deity such as this is limited by something outside his own nature and is not the source of all reality other than

4. Hick, *Philosophy of Religion*, p. 14.
5. Trueblood, *Philosophy of Religion*, p. 274.

himself. Such a deity therefore is not compatible with the definition of God accepted here.

God should neither be confused with the Pantheistic, Pluralistic, or Dualistic view of God. Often these views are compiled together when used by philosophers and theologians under the heading "Theism." Such views are not in harmony with the biblical view of God.

Having established a definition of God, we turn to the issue at stake. The question comes, "If there is a God and he is omnipotent (all-powerful) and omnibenevolent (all-loving), then why is there evil, pain, and suffering in the world? Why does God not do something about it?"

If God is a God of love, and if he is all-powerful and all-wise, how can he possibly allow so much suffering in his creation and among those he has created?

The essence of evil is evident throughout the Bible. And yet, an obvious answer is never given as to why evil exists. Many people see the essence of evil as a reason for rejecting a faith in God. The extreme difficulty is that many cannot see how God could allow evil to exist in the first place. But, granting evil's existence, then many wonder, "Why does evil *continue*? Why does God not stop it?"

Insufficient answers cause some to conclude that there is no God; for if there were, he would surely put an end to all this evil and suffering.

The problem is sometimes heightened when a look is taken at the different kinds of evil. Basically there are two:[6] Natural Evil and Moral Evil.

Natural evil (sometimes called physical evil) introduces a problem because both the guilty and the innocent suffer. Natural evil refers to those occasions in nature that cause pain and suffering. Thousands of people have been maimed or killed and untold millions of dollars worth of properties destroyed because of such tragedies as tornadoes, earthquakes, and hurricanes. Also, how can one account for the suffering brought to man from animals? A raging dog attacks a small child and as a result the child dies. Can this be called good? How can one reconcile incidents such as this with a belief in a God who is described as loving and good?

Moral evil is reconciled in most minds, because it is evil that results from man's misconduct. The specific problem of moral evil is that man commits moral evil. He is responsible for the sins he commits and is, therefore, the one to blame for the moral evil that exists. It is true that moral evil in a person's life also results in others being harmed— even though they are innocent. The only question raised here is why God allows or permits man to act in such a way.

The reality of the problem of evil and suffering must be faced. Evil and suffering are facts. Human suffering is a common denominator to man. Grief,

---

6. There are some who would list "metaphysical" evil in a category by itself, others list it under the heading "natural evil."

pain, heartache, heartbreak, trials, and tribulations exist in the lives of everyone. A search for an
adequate answer to the suffering found in the
world is a must for Christian faith. The Christian
affirms three things:[7] (1) God is good and wise. (2)
God is all-powerful and has the ability to achieve
his purposes. (3) Evil, both natural and moral, is a
fact.

The question is asked, "Why does God allow evil
to exist? If God can prevent evil, but will not, can
we say God is perfect in goodness? If he wishes to
prevent evil, but cannot, can we say that God is all-
powerful? If God has both the power and the will,
then why is evil still here?

This examination will deal with two problems:
(1) How is one to explain the origin of evil? From
where did evil come? Has evil always existed, or
was there a beginning to its existence? If there was
a beginning, when did evil begin and who is responsible for its existence in the world? (2) Given
the reality of evil's existence, why is evil allowed to
continue? Is evil a necessity to the world? And why
does the Christian suffer? Is there any value in suffering? Why does God not put a stop to evil now?
Why does he allow it to exist? Is he incapable of
stopping it? If he has the power to stop evil, why
does he not do it? These questions provoke

---

7. Stephen T. Davis expands this list with the following points : (1)
There is one God. (2) God created the world. (3) God is omnipotent.
(4) God is personal. (5) God is perfectly good. Davis, *Encountering
Evil*, p 2.

thoughts that hopefully will be covered in this study.

We will not try to prove the existence of God by looking at evil. Scripture says, "The heavens declare the glory of God" (Psalm 19:1). For the purpose of this study, we will presuppose several things. (1) There is a God who is omniscient, omnipotent, and omnibenevolent. (2) God is concerned about his creation and, in particular, man. (3) The Bible is the plenarily, verbally inspired Word of God and is the authority for all that is to be practiced in the name of religion. (4) The only real evil in the world is sin that results from man's disobedience to God's laws, and all that appears to be evil is merely man's sin.

The challenge under consideration is to reconcile a belief in the Christian God with the existence of evil. The purpose will be to discover whether or not the existence of evil in the world is, in fact, enough evidence to disprove the existence of God.[8]

Since the first edition of this book in 1976, several significant books have been published that deal with the problem of theodicy. Here I want to

---

8. This work does not try to answer the charge, "Why does not God intervene?" or, "If God can prevent such natural calamities as tornados, why doesn't he?" To respond to this would require a study of the relationship of the sovereignty of God to the problem of evil (especially natural evil). We live in a fallen world. A world where the existence of evil is the result of man's freedom of choice and the result of the original sin (Genesis 3). With Adam's sin came evil (both moral and natural). But we must remember that God is sovereign over his world and is in control of everything. There is more work that still needs to be done, and perhaps at a later time we can address this issue.

mention only a few that I think are significant for future study. I do not intend by this to say there are no others that might be of value nor that I would necessarily agree with all these authors have to say. But I think they can be read with profit by anyone interested in taking this study farther.

R.C. Sproul, *Surprised by Suffering.*

Warren W. Wiersbe, *Why Us?: When Bad Things Happen To God's People.*

Philip Yancey, *Where is God When It Hurts?* and *Disappointment with God.*

D. A. Carson, *How Long, O Lord?*

Stephen T. Davis, editor, *Encountering Evil: Live Options in Theodicy.*

Harold S. Kushner, *When Bad Things Happen To Good People.*

Stanley Hauerwas, *Naming the Silences: God, Medicine, and the Problem of Suffering.*

Michael Peterson, *Evil and the Christian God.*

Theodore Plantinga, *Learning To Live With Evil.*

A. Van De Beek, *Why? On Suffering, Guilt, and God.*

1
What's the Problem?

Good and Evil

Almost from the beginning of time, as recorded in sacred Scripture, good and evil have existed. The first portion of the book of Genesis states, "In the beginning God . . ." To speak of God is to speak of the spiritual being who has created, or brought into existence, all things past and present. During God's creative activity he created man and woman, and at the end of that creation he said, "It is very good." From that time forward, shortly after the creation of man and woman, good and evil existed in the world. The existence of evil came as a result of the fall. Man and woman sinned by being disobedient to God and, because of their sin, were driven from the garden where God placed them. The problem of good and evil plagues man with every passing year. Sometimes problems occur because of man's inability to understand why things happen.

1

It was shortly after Adam and Eve's fall in the garden that Cain killed his brother Abel. Why did Abel suffer? As God's creation, man has continually sought the answer to the problem of good and evil. Though one can somewhat understand the sorrow and cause of Adam and Eve's departure from the garden, it is difficult to understand why a person like Abel, who even though pleasing to God, must suffer. Actually, this is where the problem lies. No difficulty really stems from trying to understand why an unrighteous man, or a man who is unjust to his fellow man, would suffer. For most men believe that when the unrighteous suffer it is only just. It is deserved. The real difficulty, however, comes when the innocent suffer. Why are babies born blind and maimed and with all sorts of diseases and difficulties? Why is it that the innocent people in the world suffer? It is this problem that requires a good portion of study.

The Problem of Evil and Suffering

Why must evil and disease, and even death, exist in the world today? Why is it that people suffer? The question is often asked, "Why does God do this to me?" or, "Why does he always take away the thing that I love?" Suffering besets man from the cradle to the grave. The fact of human suffering is evident in the frightened eyes of a child and upon the brow of an old man. No creed, no color, no rank, no privilege ever escapes suffering.

The question is often asked, "Why are evil men blessed?" or, to reverse it, "Why do innocent people suffer?" Why is a promising life snuffed out as it is on the rise? Why are thousands of innocent people killed? Why are children burned, sometimes beyond recognition? Why are people lamed or maimed for life? One wonders how a God, who loves man so much, could allow suffering to come into this life.

One author has stated that there are three levels of suffering:[1] (1) the biological level, where suffering is experienced as pain; (2) the social level, which is the emotional or mental anxiety of man striving to get along with his fellow man; and (3) the moral or religious level of suffering. This level is where man struggles with the issue of why man suffers.

As the Christian approaches the problem of human suffering, he must neither deny the reality of suffering nor try to offer easy answers. The world was created by God. There is a conflict. Evil is real. It surrounds us every day. According to the Christian view, man, the creature made in God's image, is involved in this terrible, real conflict. The problems found are intense, deep, and sometimes even hideous. The problem of evil and suffering confronts man in two different ways. Intellectually man is troubled with the problem of understanding, "Why is there suffering in our world?"

---

1. Ferguson, "Problem of Evil and Suffering," p. 7.

Practically, man must cope with the problem of evil and bearing up under suffering. The question comes, "How can man do it?" Perhaps the greater of the two is the intellectual problem. The problem, therefore, is not simply *experiencing* suffering, but *understanding* it. The Christian who affirms his faith in the absolute sovereignty of God and insists that God is characterized by righteous love and goodness must reconcile this with the reality of evil in God's world. John Hick states:

> To many, the most powerful positive objection to belief in God is the fact of evil. Probably for most Agnostics it is the appalling depth and extent of human suffering, more than anything else, that makes the idea of a loving creator seem so implausible and disposes them toward one or another of the various naturalistic theories of religion.[2]

The Problem as Seen From History

The reference term often used for the attempt to reconcile the problem of pain with the justice and righteousness of God is the word "theodicy," which comes from two Greek words, *theos* (God) and *diake* (justice or righteousness). The problem of theodicy is not new. It has been discussed in detail by some of the greatest minds of the past. Plato, Augustine, Zoroaster, Mani, and others have sought to provide an answer to the problem.

---

2. Hick, *Classical and Contemporary Readings in the Philosophy of Religion,* p. 40.

The Augustinian theodicy

Augustine has been credited by some with introducing into Christian thought the doctrine of predestination and theological determinism. This has been due to his view of man's freedom of will and suffering. Georgia Harkness has stated that Augustine emphasized the omnipotence of God at the expense of man's freedom and that the most inhuman acts have been glossed over as arising from the will of God.[3]

Augustine held the belief that neither natural evil nor moral evil could be ascribed to God. He felt that it was his "duty of vindicating the Providence whose ways it seemed so seriously to impugn."[4] According to Augustine, both natural evil and moral evil had to be attributed to the will of man. Moral evil (or sin) was man's responsibility directly. Natural evil (or suffering) is a consequence of man's sin; therefore man is directly responsible. Augustine believed that all evil (including suffering), which is not identical to sin, is derived from or is a punishment for sin. This raises the question, "For whose sin does one suffer?" Augustine viewed natural evil (suffering) as a punishment for the sin of Adam. Every individual was a participant in that sin of Adam. The thesis of Augustine was twofold: (1) "All human nature existed as a mass in

---

3. Harkness, *Conflicts in Religious Thought*, p. 234.
4. Fairbairn, *Philosophy of Christian Religion*, p. 234.

Adam."[5] (2) "We all were in that one man, since we were part of that one man who fell into sin."[6]

The theodicy of Leibniz

G. W. Leibniz (1646-1716) was a mathematician and rationalistic philosopher who produced a monumental work on evil and suffering entitled *Theodicee*. In it he endeavors to justify God's dealings with men as they relate to the evils of life. Leibniz was influenced by Augustine, but always maintained that he was not bound by Augustine's concepts. His main thesis was that imperfection is a rational necessity in a finite world. His formula properly stated is as follows: "This is the best of all possible worlds."[7]

To Leibniz, nature did not exist by necessity. Nature might or might not have been, and it was because God so determined it to be. A better world might be imagined by someone, but no better world could have been made than was made.

It was the contention of Leibniz that "evil is due to the necessary limitation imposed by the good and holy God by the fact that he is dealing with finite things."[8] This rationalization became a criterion for Leibniz for affirming not only metaphysical imperfection (such as blindness or disease), but also imperfection in the form of pain and sin.

---

5. Augustine, "The Confessions," p. 14.
6. Augustine, "The City of God," p. 14.
7. Fairbairn, *Philosophy of Christian Religion*, p. 104.
8. Nevius, *Religion as Experience and Truth*, p. 337.

Natural evil (suffering), he argued, is inherent to finite existence. He felt that God could not have created a world without suffering. It was possible that God could have created more evil than is present, but his goodness would not allow it. Being perfect in goodness, then, God could not avoid creating the best possible world. When God created the world, he did so as free from evil as could possibly be allowed. It is understood from Leibniz that it is the "divine reason, therefore, that 'constitutes the principle of evil.'"[9] Essentially, Leibniz's theodicy fulfills the same function as Adam's sin to Augustine's theodicy. It exempts God from the responsibility for the evils of the world.

Royce's theodicy

Josiah Royce (1855-1916), Professor of Philosophy at Harvard College, attempted to solve the problem of evil and suffering. It was his contention that the suffering found in the world was in existence because suffering is found in the essential nature of God. He believed that God suffers with man, and that man's sufferings are God's sufferings. He says,

> God is not in ultimate essence other being than yourself. He is the Absolute Being. You truly are one with God, part of his life. He is the very soul of your soul. And so, here is the

---

9. Knudson, *Basic Issues*, p. 95.

first truth: when you suffer, your sufferings are God's sufferings.[10]

But why does God suffer in this way? "Because without suffering, without ill, without woe, evil, tragedy, God's life could not be perfected."[11] According to this, God is made perfect through suffering and suffering is what makes him perfect. This same principle applies to human suffering.

According to Royce, suffering is essential to the perfection of the universe.

Theodicy of Dualism

The answer of Dualism to the problem of theodicy is based in a denial of the omnipotence of God. This explanation for suffering says that suffering exists because God does not have the power to prevent it. This is sometimes referred to as the philosophy of dualism or pluralism. Basically, the theory says that good and evil are two coeternal principles that war against each other. From such a belief comes the teaching of the finiteness of God.

Pluralistic approaches have taken different forms in the history of philosophy. The struggle between light and darkness is evidenced in the dualistic teachings of Zoroastrianism and

---

10. From Josiah Royce, *Studies in Good and Evil*, pp. 13-28. Original publications, 1898, by D. Appleton and Company. In The Public Domain as cited by Abernathy and Langeford in "The Problem of Job," *Philosophy of Religion,* p. 398.

11. Ibid.

Manichaeism. Zoroaster, who lived in Persia (circa 1000 B.C.), said there were two gods, Ahura Mazdeh (good) and Angra Mainyu (evil), who fought against each other. Zoroaster called on men to join the battle by fighting with Ahura Mazdeh against Angra Mainyu. Another thought similar to this comes from the thinking of Mani (circa A.D. 215) often called Manichaeism.[12]

In the area of philosophy Plato says,

> God is a friend to man and an enemy to evil. Since God is finite, the conflict with evil is real and since the receptacle is unchanging and timeless, the conflict with evil is everlasting. God takes sides in a battle of which the outcome is not a foreordained victory for his side.[13]

The problem that dualism must face is that the conflict is described as everlasting. Where then is there a hope of good coming from evil? One of the most accepted doctrines of dualism is the belief of a finite God. The teaching of a finite God is based on an empirical conviction that there is a sufficient amount of evil in the world to grant the conclusion that God is finite in power. According to this, "A God infinite in both goodness and power could not have permitted such things in nature as the birth of idiots and the unruly massacring of the innocent by natural evil."[14]

---

12. Cf. Hick, *Evil and the God of Love*, pp. 29-31.
13. Raphael, *The Philosophy of Plato,* p. 287.
14. Ibid.

J. S. Mill and external dualism

John Stuart Mill (1806-1873) did not accept the traditional Christian belief in a God who, as creator of the world, could be described as omnipotent and omnibenevolent.

> It is not too much to say that every indication of Design in the Kosmos is so much evidence against the Omnipotence of the Designer. For what is meant by Design? Contrivance: the adaption of means to an end. But the necessity for contrivance—the need of employing means—is a consequence of the limitation of power. Who would have recourse to means if to attain his end mere word were sufficient? The very idea of means implies that the means have an efficacy which the direct action of the being who employs them has not. . . . But if the employment of contrivance is itself a sign of limited power, how much more so is the careful and skilful choice of contrivance? . . . Wisdom and contrivance are shown in overcoming difficulties and there is no room for them in a Being for whom no difficulties exist. The evidences, therefore, of Natural Theology distinctly imply that the author of the Kosmos worked under limitations; that he was obligated to adapt himself to conditions independent of his will, and to attain his ends by such arrangements as those conditions admitted of.[15]

---

15. Mill, *Three Essays on Religion,* (London: Longmans, Green, Reader & Dyer, 1875), "Theism: Attributes," pp. 176-77, as cited by Hick, *Evil and the God of Love,* p. 34.

Mill went on to say that the evil in nature is the result of a malfunctioning system of the universe that was basically designed to preserve and enhance life. He stated that there is no ground in Natural Theology for ascribing intelligence or personality to obstacles which partially thwart the purposes of God. The fact that the obstacles were there was evidence to Mill that God was limited and therefore finite.

Regarding Mill's view, John Hick says:

> Mill does not say how this view is to be applied to moral evil. He is not willing to postulate a devil, as a personal malevolent power who could be regarded as the instigator of human sin; nor does he suggest any other explanation of its origin. Presumably he would have to hold that matter and energy, together with the laws of their operation, as the circumstances that God has not created and with which he has to contend, somehow necessitate man's moral frailty and failure.[16]

E. S. Brightman and internal dualism

Edgar S. Brightman (1884-1953) offers one of the most significant thoughts to the theory of a finite God. Brightman maintained that the limitation of God was internal, that is, within himself, rather than external, with man. Brightman has been perhaps the greatest contemporary contender for the proposition that God is finite.

---

16. Hick, *Evil and the God of Love*, p. 34.

Traditional Christian theism has held that God voluntarily limits himself in his dealings with his finite creatures. Brightman explains this by saying that within the divine will there is a restriction imposed by "the Given" which resists the divine will and prevents man from being free from suffering. He says:

> The Given consists of the eternal uncreated laws of reason and also of equally eternal processes of nonrational consciousness which exhibit all the ultimate qualities of sense objects (*qualia*), disorderly impulses and desires, such experiences as pain and suffering, the forms of space and time, and whatever in God is the source of surd evil.[17]

By "surd evil" he means "objects, events, or experiences that are intrinsically and irredeemably evil and incapable of being turned to good."[18] Brightman ascribes "surd evil" to God when he says that "there is something in God which is the *source of surd evil.*"[19]

Brightman is saying that suffering and pain cannot be attributed to a wholly good God. Somewhere God's divine will must have been turned from its course. Since there is no power outside of or independent of God from which this could

---

17. Brightman, *A Philosophy of Religion*, p. 337.
18. Hick, *Evil and the God of Love*, p. 37.
19. Brightman, *A Philosophy of Religion*, p.337, (italics added).

have come, it must have come from something within the divine nature itself; this he calls "the Given."

The Nature of Evil

How does a person describe evil? Basically, there are two types of evil, natural and moral. Though a more detailed examination will be given of these at a later time, a brief view will be given of both at this point.

Natural evil

Natural evil includes all the frustrations of human values which are perpetrated, not by the free agency of man, but by natural elements in the universe. This would include such things as hurricanes, tornadoes, wind storms, hail storms, disease, and birth defects. Any event that happens within nature itself and causes destruction on man is referred to as a natural evil. Natural evils perhaps cause the greatest difficulties for many people, because when they happen the question is always raised, "Is God not unfair in his dealings?" In the words of John Mill,

> Killing, the most criminal act recognized by human laws, nature does once to every being that lives and in a large proportion of cases, after protracted torture such as only the greatest monsters whom we read of ever purposely inflicted on their living fellow

creatures . . . nature impales men, breaks them as if on the wheel, casts them to be devoured by the wild beast, burns them to death, crushes them with stones like the first Christian martyr, starves them with hunger, freezes them with cold. . . . All this nature does with the most supercilious disregard, both of mercy and justice, emptying her shafts upon the best and the noblest indifferently with the meanest and the worst.[20]

A large reason why natural evil is particularly a problem to the Christian is that Christianity says not only that all of nature was created by the Almighty, but that it was pronounced by him to be very good. Christians are also told that the very present movement of all things is guided and guarded by the watchful eye of the one who accomplishes all things according to the counsel of his will (Ephesians 1:11). A loved one goes on a trip and, in a tragic accident, loses his life. In such a case no human being would be accused of foreseeing the tragedy and yet permitting the injury to happen anyway. Being finite in power, human beings do not foresee such tragedies. But with God such is not the case, and here lies the problem. Can a Christian walk through this world and see the calamities that befall man without asking "Why?"

---

20. John Stuart Mill, *Three Essays on Religion*, p. 28, as quoted by Carnell, *Introduction to Christian Apologetics*, pp. 280-81.

Moral evil

It is said that moral evil includes all those frustrations of human value which are perpetrated, not by the natural elements of the universe, but by the free agency of man himself. Many people would say that moral evils are worse than physical evils. Though they may not be as physically painful, they nonetheless carry great sufferings.

> Mental evils are worse than physical, though perhaps not as immediately painful, for though one can move from the path of an impending hurricane, he cannot outrun either the judgment of the conscience within or the fear of the course of things without. As to the latter fear, all our struggles, all our hopes, seemed destined to destruction and that which befalls the son of man befalls beasts. Even one thing befalls them, as the one dies so does the other. Yea, they all have one breath. . . . All are of one dust and all turn to dust again (Ecclesiastes 3:19-20).[21]

So man is perplexed. He worries. This causes anxiety. Anxiety brings fear, and fear often brings trouble. When these come, they bring distress in insecurity, neurosis, and lust. The security of a century's work is dashed by the mad ambitions of one who wants to dictate. Or, the retirement provisions of an old person are lost in a depression, and the

---

21. Carnell, *Introduction to Christian Apologetics*, p. 282.

institutions in which man has lately placed his faith collapse.

Moral evil is a problem. Despite the fact that man causes much, if not all, moral evil, the question is, "Why did God, who could have done otherwise, make man so that he is vulnerable to the threats of worry, distress, and fear?" It is said of Descartes that he

> sagaciously remarked that a proof for his dependence upon God was that if he had made Descartes, he would have done a different job. But why did not God do that job with us in the first place? We seem able potentially to enjoy happiness—why do we not actually do so?[22]

The Nature of the Problem of Evil and Suffering

From the days of Epicurus, Lactantius, and others, there have been discussions on the problem of evil and human suffering. In its various forms, the essence of what is said is this: either God wants to prevent evil and he cannot do it, or he can prevent evil but does not want to, or he neither wishes to nor can prevent evil, or he wishes to and can prevent it. The point is, if God has the desire without the power, he is impotent; if he can but does not desire to, he has a malice that cannot be attributed

---

22. Ibid.

to God. If God has neither the power nor the desire, he is both impotent and evil and, therefore, not God. If he has the desire and the power to prevent evil, then where did evil come from initially and why does God not prevent it now?

The force of the argument in the words of David Hume is as follows:

> Let us assume that God exists, is omnibenevolent (all-good), omniscient (all-knowing), and omnipotent (all-powerful). If he is omnibenevolent, it is often suggested that he is always willing to prevent evil. If he is omniscient, he knows how to do so. If he is omnipotent, then he can do so. Hence, if God exists then evil does not. But evil plainly does exist. So God does not exist.[23]

In a treatise on the anger of God, Lactantius, a fourth-century Christian apologist, explains the problem in his words as he alludes to the view of Epicurus, when he says,

> God . . . either wishes to take away evils and is unable or he is able and is unwilling or he is neither willing nor able or he is both willing and able. If he is willing and unable, he is feeble, which is not in accordance with the character of God. If he is able and unwilling, he is envious, which is equally at variance with God. If he is neither willing nor able, he is both envious and feeble and, therefore, not

23. As quoted by Yandell, *Basic Issues in the Philosophy of Religion*, p. 43.

God. If he is both willing and able, which alone is suitable to God, from what source then are evils, or why does he not remove them?[24]

According to David Hume, the existence of evil in the world makes a belief in God illogical and incompatible. He quotes Philo in answer to the question raised of misery and human suffering. Why does God not do something about all the evil and suffering in the world? He argues:

> His [God's] power we allow infinite: whatever he wills is executed: but neither man nor any other animal is happy: therefore he does not will their happiness. His wisdom is infinite: he is never mistaken in choosing the means to any end: but the course of nature tends not to human or animal felicity: therefore it is not established for that purpose.[25]

Philo continues his argument when he says,

> Epicurus's old questions are yet unanswered. Is he willing to prevent evil, but not able? Then he is impotent. Is he able but not willing? Then he is malevolent. Is he both able and willing? Whence then is evil?[26]

---

24. Lactantius, "A Treatise on the Anger of God," as cited by Roberts in *The Ante-Nicene Fathers*, p. 271.
25. As quoted by Warren, *Have Atheists Proved There Is No God?*, p. 5.
26. Ibid.

Such a statement has Philo affirming that belief in a God who is both omnipotent and omnibenevolent is a logical contradiction. If it is true that God is omnibenevolent, then he should want all men to be happy. If he is omnipotent, then he has the power to make all men happy. But there are some men who are not happy; therefore, some conclude that (1) God is either not omnibenevolent or not omnipotent, or (2) he is neither omnipotent nor omnibenevolent.[27]

The Christian teaches that God is all-good and all-powerful. And yet every day there are facts that seem to deny such statements, thus putting doubt in many people's minds. Is it logical that man can believe there is a God that is sovereign, both in goodness and power, when in the universe it is a fact that many righteous people suffer and many wicked people prosper? We live in a universe, as Augustine said, "where the organic parts of a flea are marvelously fitted and framed, while human life is surrounded and made restless by the inconsistency of countless disorders."[28]

In searching for an answer to such questions raised by this problem, perhaps the Christian's first temptation is to say that the problem of evil is a mystery. But such a thought as this tends to limit faith by supposing it to be a cessation of the mind

---

27. Ibid., pp. 5-6.
28. Augustine, "De Ordine," I, 1, 2; as quoted by Carnell, *Introduction to Christian Apologetics*, p. 278.

because of insufficient evidence. Some men have
been content to confess the mystery of evil and to
say it is unexplainable. But that is not true of modern man. Unlike people of yesteryear, the contemporary mind delights in raising and pressing all
issues which pertain in any way to the nature and
the destiny of man. James Orr says:

> Man will think on those deep problems which
> lie at the root of religious belief—on the
> nature of God, his character, his relations to
> the world and men, sin, the means of deliver-
> ance from it, the end to which all things are
> moving—and if Christianity does not give
> them an answer suited to their deeper and
> more reflective moods, they will simply put it
> aside as inadequate for their needs.[29]

With the teaching of uniformitarianism and the
theory of evolution, man has begun to think of himself as the final product, as all there really is.
Therefore man has been in a quest to make this
world the best world possible, which has occupied a
greater portion of his time. Man has sought in this
age of technological knowledge to become sensitive
to every organized way of nature and to try to do
everything possible to control the processes of the
natural world to make this world the best world
possible. In the religious world, Modernism, with
all its forces, has completely left out the funda-

---

29. Orr, *Christian View of God and the World*, p. 21.

mental concepts of faith. As long as man seemed to be getting better and better, it was supposed that the evil which found its way in man was simply something that resulted from brute ancestry. It is rather obvious, though, that the wars, trials, tribulations, heartaches, and other catastrophes that man faces today point to the fact that man's inner nature is evil. It is true that things have not worked out as man had always planned. Though man has continued his argument for greater advancement of knowledge and technology, man can become a morally revolting monster. Evil is written on the heart and inner nature of man so deeply that even human history itself is filled with the elements of man's own destruction.

This dissatisfaction that Modernism and Liberalism have given to the world has caused, at least to some extent, modern man to agree with the teachings of Christianity, that there is a problem of evil in the world. The tragedy involved is that modern man rejects the solution that Christianity offers to the problem, namely, that there is an infinitely powerful, good God, and that he is the author of all things. As Carnell states, man today would say that

> an infinitely powerful, good God cannot be the author of nature and all its parts. For in sober truth, nearly all things for which men are hanged or imprisoned for doing to one another, are nature's everyday performances.[30]

---

30. Carnell, *Introduction to Christian Apologetics*, p. 280.

The Origin of Evil[31]

One important question in this study is "Whence does evil come?" Does evil originate with God? Did God create evil? Isaiah 45:6-7 reads,

> *I am Jehovah, and there is none else. I form the light, and create darkness; I make peace and create evil; I am Jehovah that doeth all these things.*

From this passage of Scripture, many have concluded that God created evil. After all, is that not exactly what the passage says?

As Isaiah looked around him, he saw idolatry in the form of polytheism. The people of the land believed in many gods and had an idol created for each god. Jehovah had already challenged the idol's ability against his own (43:21-24). In 45:20 the prophet says that the people "carry the wood of their graven image." Isaiah tells the people that there are not many gods, as they depict by their many idols, but only one God, Jehovah, and that he created all things.

---

31. In discussing the origin of evil, the author is not making a distinction between natural evil and moral evil. While there is a valid distinction between the two, the concern of this section is over the problem of origin. Where did evil (and through evil, suffering) begin? My conclusion is that the origin of evil is outside man and, therefore, must be recognized for there to be an understanding of the Fall and its impact on man and his world.

Dualism is at the front of the battle. Cyrus, king of Persia (to whom the forty-fifth chapter of Isaiah is addressed) had been under the instruction of the false preacher Zoroaster. This false preacher said that the world was composed of two parts, evenly balanced against each other. One was supposedly good, the other evil. One was light, the other darkness. Isaiah says there is only one God, and he is the creator of all things. There are not two gods fighting against each other, but only one God and he is supreme, infinite and exalted above all things. Using language from that vantage point, the prophet says there is only one God and that he made the darkness as well as the light, evil as well as good. Isaiah did not want the people of God to fall into the belief of the Persians that darkness was as strong as light or that evil was as great a force as good. The thought is that there is only one great God, Jehovah, and he is over everything.

Granting the absolute sovereignty of God, is one forced to believe that God created evil? If God is the absolute sovereign over all things, then evil could not be here unless it comes from God. How can one answer?

One answer given is that when God made man, he made him with the freedom of choice. Man could choose either good or evil. Man is not a mere robot or automaton. He is a free moral being, different from all of God's creation. Machines or robots can do almost anything if they are programmed to do so. But that is the point; they must be programmed in order to do it. Their actions are predetermined. They can never do anything except what they have been programmed to do. God could have made man that way, but where would be the glory? It would be gone, because man would respond in exactly the same way every time. The glory of the freedom of choice that man enjoys would be absent.

After giving a biblical view of sin, James Orr asks, "How such an act should ever originate may again be a problem we cannot solve; *but it is evidently included in the possibilities of human freedom.*"[32]

This question may also be raised: "If man were a mere automaton, where would be the glory in heroism or self-sacrifice?" In a time of danger, a person tries to do the impossible, and it costs him his life. We talk about his heroic example. Such language would be useless if freedom of choice were not involved. When God made man, he made him with the ability to choose the bad as well as the good. In that sense, God made the world so that evil is in it.

Another answer often given is that God created evil in the sense that he made a world that operates on the basis of laws. When these laws are broken, calamity follows. Sorrow and pain are natural results of sin. The evil that God creates is the calamity, woe, and disaster that come as the result

---

32. Orr, *Christian View of God and the World*, p. 172, (italics added).

of evil choice. The world God made is one in which there are consequences resulting from wrongdoing.

Pursuing the question further, one may ask whether evil comes from Satan. Receiving an affirmative answer, he then asks, "But whence comes Satan?"[33]

The dual problem of sin and Satan has long been the discussion of philosophers and theologians alike. When a person thinks of sin, his mind goes back to the garden where sin first entered the human race. However, sin's origin was not there, but prior to that time. Sin's origin traces back not to men, but to angels; it began not on earth, but in heaven. It is generally accepted that Satan was once an angel who, because of his rebellion, was cast out of heaven. Two passages of Scripture often referred to regarding Satan's early history are Ezekiel 28:11-19 and Isaiah 14:12-14. Of Ezekiel 28:11-19 one writer says that

> while the prophecy or statements of this passage are addressed to the person named, they appear to go beyond an earthly monarch and can only apply to a supernatural being of some kind. Ezekiel, talking of contemporaneous events, goes beyond them, and using them as a type, goes from a reference to the king of Tyre to Satan, of whom the king is a type. Before he sinned, or iniquity was found in him, Satan was known as Lucifer.[34]

33. For an abbreviated study of the Fall of Satan, I would suggest: Edward P. Myers, *A Study of Angels*, chapter 8.

34. Lockyer, *All the Doctrines of the Bible*, p. 134.

To many, this seems to be the most plausible explanation, as it gives a double meaning to the prophecy and still preserves the conviction that this passage refers to the origin of Satan. He continues, "'Thou wast perfect in all thy ways from the day thou wast created.' Here is the simple explanation of the true origin of the angelic being who became the devil."[35]

Referring to the Isaiah passage, the same author says that

> Lucifer became Satan when he tried to make himself not only equal with God, but as one above God. Note the fivefold personal pronoun I. Covetous, he would not be satisfied with anything short of the very highest position in God's original creation. Pride preceded his overthrow (Proverbs 16:18). The middle letter of pride is I, just as it is in sin, and it was the big I that brought about the fall of the divinely created anointed cherub. He sinned against divine sovereignty and was thus cast out of heaven (Isaiah 14:13,14; 2 Thessalonians 2:4-9) . . . . Many of the angels likewise revolted against God and aspired to divine authority, and followed Lucifer as their recognized head (Matthew 9:34; 25:41; Ephesians 2:2).[36]

Another says, "In their full scope these passages paint Satan's past career as 'Lucifer' and as 'The Anointed Cherub' in his pre-fall splendor."[37]

---

35. Ibid.
36. Ibid., p. 135.
37. Unger, "Satan," p. 472.

Regardless of the debate over the meaning of these passages, the existence of Satan is real. Scripture presents him as a real being who is the archenemy of God. Satan is pictured as the one who is ultimately responsible for such evil as murder. It is said of him that he was a murderer "from the beginning" (John 8:44). He holds the power of death (Hebrews 2:14), but has been conquered by Christ. His final outcome is pictured in Revelation 20:1-15.

Evil, then, had its beginning before time. Satan, a created being from heaven, rebelled against the creator. Having been judged because of this rebellion, he desires to devour God's creation by tempting man to reject his creator.

The Continued Existence of Evil

Another important question for our study is "Why does God not put a stop to evil now?" Is it fair for God to allow people, innocent people, to suffer if he has the power to prevent it? Or, does he have the power to prevent it? Perhaps the reason God does not prevent evil is that he is powerless to do so. This is the answer that Finitism gives when it says God is finite and powerless to prevent evil.

The continued existence of evil in the world is allowed by God for at least one reason. God will not force man to do that which man (of his own freedom of will) chooses not to do. Evil is in existence today because God allows man freedom of choice, even if that freedom involves disobedience to God.

The answer to the problem of the continued existence of evil comes from the inquiry, "Why does God not stop evil and suffering now?" A sufficient answer is found in the word "redemption." The Bible reveals the complete sovereignty of God and his governing the world. Man has sinned against God, and because he has done so, evil is in the world. But evil is overcome (in the final analysis) by God through the sacrifice of Jesus Christ. A time is coming when God will put an end to all the evil that is in the world. Satan and all the forces of evil will be brought to eternal judgment. In the meantime, God's grace and mercy are extended to man to cause him to cease doing evil and live in a right relationship with God.

God has done the most drastic thing that could be done in dealing with evil. He gave his son to die on the cross that man might escape the judgment that is to come on sin and evil. The final solution, therefore, to the continued existence of evil is found in Jesus Christ.

Suggested Solutions

As man ponders the problems and difficulties involved in the existence of evil, what kind of answers are found? Are there really any answers? Is man left hopeless and helpless without any logical reason for why evil is here? Are there any real answers?

Many people suggest answers. One suggests that the problem of evil is overexaggerated, that evil is not really the difficulty or problem some people make it out to be. Evil just tends to be in existence because of many various dispositions. Another says that evil's presence is just a stimulation to do good, because if we did not have evil to contrast with good, how would we really know how to appreciate that which is good? Without any temptation or danger, all courage and all honor would fail. Still others argue that evil is merely an earthly problem. But could such suggestions actually offer consolation in face of the fact that there is evil in our world and that people do suffer? If there is no real evidence, no rational evidence for the Christian doctrine of man's relationship to God as it has existed from the beginning until now, then faith must be abandoned.

Various alternatives exist for the person who concludes that there is a problem of evil. (1) A person can deny the reality of evil. This is often done in Pantheism. One defines God as all, and all as God. Therefore, evil is simply an illusion. By approaching the difficulty this way, evil is merely discarded by denying its true reality. (2) A person can say that evil is real and God is real and that they are merely two different eternal principles that have always struggled against one another and will forever continue to do so. Such is the view of Plato. Often, this way of approaching the problem of evil is referred to as Dualism. That is, there are two ultimate principles in reality. (3) A man can state that God sovereignly decreed the present universe and, in doing so, permitted the entrance of evil into it to fulfill those purposes elected by him to be fulfilled in Christianity. This is a view often referred to as Theism, a philosophy that teaches that God is both transcendent and immanent and declares that from eternity there was only good and no evil. For the Theist, evil is either sin or the punishment for sin or the consequence of sin, and its value is disciplinary.

In order to better understand the nature of the problem of evil and suffering, it is necessary to make a distinction between natural evil and moral evil. Such a distinction is the subject of the following two chapters.

2

What on Earth Is Wrong?

The Problem of Natural Evil

Unbelievers claim they can prove that the God of the Bible does not exist. The question is whether there is sufficient evidence for such a conclusion.

The charge made with greater frequency than any other against biblical theism is that such theism cannot adequately explain the occurrence or existence of evil. Many rule out the idea of biblical theism that presents God as omnipotent and omnibenevolent on the basis of the far-reaching effect of evil, pain, and human suffering. Evil, as viewed by such men, presents sufficient cause for them to reject biblical theism and to select, as an alternative, Atheism or a naturalistic theory of religion.

The purpose of this chapter is to discuss the problem of natural evil as it relates to the Christian belief in a God who is described as om-nipotent and omnibenevolent. *First*, there is a dis-tinction made between the two types of evil (natu-ral evil and moral evil). The emphasis of this chapter will be on natural evil, and the following chapter will deal with moral evil. *Second* is a dis-cussion of the subject of the goodness of God and the problem of natural evil. *Third*, there is an en-larged discussion of the problem of natural evil with a presentation of objections to a belief in God because of the existence of natural evil. Along with these objections will be an appraisal showing strengths and weaknesses of the objections. *Fourth*, a series of answers to the problem of natu-ral evil that have been presented by various au-thors are listed with an evaluation of each answer. *Finally*, there will be a summary of the answers given and a presentation of the solutions that are here judged to be important and acceptable.

Two Types of Evil

Any attempt to discuss the problem of evil must begin by distinguishing between the two types of evil, namely, natural evil and moral evil. Natural evil[1] refers to events in nature that cause pain and

---

1. Other names are used for natural evil. Authors vary in their de-scription of this subject. Some refer to "natural evil" as "physical evil" or "nonmoral evil." In any case, all these terms refer to the same thing.

suffering, but which are not a result of man's choice; they simply happen. Under this heading fall natural events such as tornadoes, floods, hurricanes, hailstorms, earthquakes, and disastrous consequences which are not necessarily the result of anyone's wrongdoing. Natural evils are not a result of acts or dispositions of the human will. Many result from natural causes, which operate according to laws that God has put in force in the world. Because these evils bring pain and suffering to man, the problem of natural evil is one of the major forms of the problem of evil.

Distinction is necessary

Although there is a distinction that should be made between the two kinds of evil, confusion often arises because of their relationship to each other. Natural evils sometimes result from natural causes, but sometimes they are caused by human acts (or failures to act) and the moral factors involved. Rapidly melting snow or heavy rains can cause floods, but in some cases these disasters could have been avoided by building higher and stronger dams or by diverting the water in the rivers from their usual courses. A stomachache is the result of a physiological cause, but it might have been effected by overeating. A famine might be due to the failure of fields to produce an adequate supply, but a change in methods of farming might have avoided the problem. In such ways as these, man causes many natural evils. However, natural causes are often among the conditions, if they are sufficient causes, of some of the moral evils found in our world.

Distinction is important

To some it might seem that the distinction made between natural and moral evil makes the problem of evil even more complex. Yet, it is very important to distinguish them from one another, because they raise different problems which must be answered in different ways.

Elton Trueblood states:

> Natural evil is far less important in the modern world than moral evil, but it is harder to explain. It is relatively easy to see, once the case is made, that to expect personality without its high price is to expect absurdity, but this will not explain natural evils. It helps to explain suffering in a concentration camp, but it will not explain suffering from an eruption of a volcano. We can agree that God needed to give us costly freedom if He desired to make us real persons, but why did He need to make earthquakes?[2]

Are there adequate answers for the questions raised from natural disasters? If so, what are they? If there are adequate answers, why does the debate continue?

If physical suffering were inflicted upon a person every time he did something wrong, and only then,

2. Trueblood, *Philosophy of Religion*, p. 253.

it would not be difficult to understand or explain. It would be visible proof of a supreme power. But the charge is made that physical suffering is meaningless and contributes nothing to the betterment of our world. Also, it often seems as if the innocent suffer most. How can this be reconciled with the Christian belief in a God described as omnibenevolent?

The Goodness of God

When the Christian appeals to the Bible as the basis for speaking of the goodness of God, he is likely to encounter fallacious charges. To some people, what is recorded in the Bible seems far from "good."

John W. Wenham, who believes in the goodness of God, presents the problem from the unbeliever's viewpoint:

> The book contains many horrors. There is tyranny, cruelty, mutilation—eyes gouged out, hands lopped off—deceit, licentiousness, war. Not only war, but God-sent war. Assyria, one of the cruellest nations of history, is called the rod of God's anger. God is angry and wreaks vengeance. A man here is struck blind, another dumb, another is covered with leprosy, another falls down dead, another dies in agony, another goes mad. Whole populations are devastated by plague or famine or flood or fire and brimstone. With God's full permission, the Devil and a host of other powerful

and malevolent spirits stalk the earth, tempting and tormenting man, even to depriving an innocent man of health and wealth and family. There are cursing psalms. There are terrible pictures of hell, in which a man craves water to cool the tip of his tongue, and in which the smoke of torment rises from a lake of fire. There is war on earth and a war in heaven and a war in the human heart.

Lord Platt, writing in *The Times* about the New English Bible said,

Perhaps now that it is written in a language all can understand the Old Testament can be seen for what it is, an obscene chronicle of man's cruelty to man, or worse perhaps, his cruelty to woman, and of man's selfishness and cupidity backed up by his appeal to his god; a horror story if ever there was one. It is hoped that it will at last be proscribed as totally inappropriate to the ethical instruction of schoolchildren.[3]

The Problem of Natural Evil

Norman Geisler poses the problem of natural evil in these terms:

Perhaps the best known statement of the problem of physical evil is in *Camus' Plague*. Speaking about a plague of rats visited upon the city of Oran at the beginning of the second world war, Camus insisted that:

_____
3. Wenham, *The Goodness of God*, pp. 7-8.

1. Either one must join the doctor and fight the plague or else join the priest and not fight the plague.
2. But not to fight the plague is anti-humanitarian.
3. And to fight the plague is to fight against God who sent it.
4. Therefore, if humanitarianism is right, Theism is wrong.
5. Humanitarianism is right.
6. Therefore, God is wrong.[4]

Geisler summarizes an article by H. J. McCloskey, entitled "God and Evil," and says the severity of the dilemma for the believer in God in the face of the problem of natural evil is as follows:

1. The Theist is morally obligated to promote the greatest good.
2. The greatest good cannot be achieved by eliminating suffering (according to Theism) for—
   a. if the necessary condition for achieving something is eliminated, then the possibility of achieving that something is eliminated,
   b. and, eliminating evils would (according to Theism) eliminate the necessary condition for achieving a greater good;
   c. hence, the greatest good cannot be achieved by eliminating suffering.

4. Geisler, *Philosophy of Religion*, pp. 380-81.

    3. Therefore, the Theist is morally obligated (in accordance with his own thesis) not to work to eliminate evil.[5]

It is with the problem thus stated that one really enters into the arena and fights the battle. Geisler summarizes the arguments against Theism from natural evil in this way:

    1. If suffering is justifiable, it is wrong to work against it.
    2. It is not wrong to work to eliminate suffering (it is right to do so).
    3. Hence, suffering is not justifiable.
    4. But if evil is not justifiable, then the Theistic God does not exist.
    5. For God's existence is incompatible with unjustifiable suffering.
    6. And there is unjustifiable suffering (from premise three above).
    7. Therefore, the Theistic God cannot exist.[6]

Here is where the problem really lies. If suffering brings about a condition that enables man to experience a greater good, then man should not work to eliminate suffering, lest he be working to eliminate the greater good. Now if suffering or a plague is sent from God to punish man and man works to eliminate that suffering or that plague, then man is found guilty of working directly against God. Whether suffering is a condition for

5. Ibid.
6. Ibid., pp. 381-82.

achieving a greater good or a consequence of doing evil, man is working against a greater good by working against suffering. This makes a belief in God inhuman.

Once a man has established the existence of God to his satisfaction, his religious problems begin anew. Questions are then raised concerning the character of this God. It could well be that this supreme being does exist, but what if this being were basically evil or impotent? The possibility that this might be the case arises whenever man is faced with the natural catastrophes which are in the world. Diseases unnumbered lay waste the physical and mental powers of man. Difficulties are caused by hurricanes, floods, tornadoes, and all such catastrophes that destroy the material advances which man makes, removing either life itself or the means by which life could have been maintained. Man begins to wonder whether the God he has just established may not be more of a cosmic tyrant, or a universal sadist, rather than a God of omnipotence and omnibenevolence. How to save the character of God in the presence of all the natural evils is what has been discussed as "the problem of natural evil." There are two premises in this study that are assumed: (1) There are events harmful to man which are not caused by man. These events are not rare and exceptional, but widespread and common; they are found in man's everyday life. (2) There is an infinite God. The minimum characteristics which this God possesses are omnipotence, omniscience, and omnibenevolence.

Solutions Offered to the Problem

A number of solutions have been proposed as a means of answering the problem of both the origin and the continued existence of natural evil. Any one of these by itself are not to be taken as final. Whether any one is valid or not will not be discussed at the moment. They are simply being listed. These proposed solutions are as follows:

1. Man's freedom grants the possibility of natural evil.

There are natural evils, and yet there is an infinite God who possesses the minimum characteristics of being omniscient, omnipotent, and omnibenevolent. Man's free will is basic to human morality. It is here that J. L. Mackie, Professor of Philosophy, University College, Oxford, England, raises his objection. Dr. Mackie says the belief in a God described as omnipotent and wholly good presents a logical contradiction because there is pain, evil, and suffering in the world.

He says that if God could have made man in such a way as he would always choose the good on one of several occasions, then he could have also made man to choose the good on every occasion. To Mackie, God could have made man to act freely without interfering with man's freedom. Mackie says that man could have been made to act freely, but in acting freely, always make the right choice. Since God could have done this but did not do so, he is inconsistent with his being both omnipotent and wholly good.[7]

Dr. Mackie fails to realize that when God made man in his image, he gave man a freedom like that which he himself enjoyed. Hubert Black notes:

> If man had not been free, he could not be described as being in the image of God. God is free to will, to act, to do as he may please; the instant you imply any limitation on him, you cease to think of him as God.[8]

His freedom is a genuine freedom and involves the freedom of choice. Man is an independent being and can exercise his freedom either with or against his creator. If man did not have the freedom to choose, then the praise and devotion he gives to God would have no meaning. Man's being given the freedom to make his own choices also implies the reality of moral responsibility.

Granted, the problem of freedom of will is difficult for some to discern. However, no theist can hold that man is simply an automaton that acts at the direction of another (even God) without his own consent or will. God placed Adam and Eve in the Garden of Eden. He allowed them to enjoy the

---

7. Mackie, "Evil and Omnipotence."
8. Black, *Good God! Cry or Credo?*, p. 43.

world he had created for them. Man is pictured in
this state as being blessed with the powers of reason and choice. Being able to choose between good
and evil makes man free in the widest sense of the
term. The fact is that God did not make man a puppet. God could have made man a puppet had he so
desired. He could have made man perfect and without the ability to rebel against him. If God had
wanted to, he could have created man unable to
sin. But then man would not be described as man
the way he is known today, that is, having the
quality of freedom of choice. God made man in his
image and in his likeness, and in doing so, he gave
man freedom to choose for himself.

John Wenham says that

> the endowing of man with freedom of choice
> involves the possibility (in God's foreknowl-
> edge, the certainty) of sin in all its horror. Yet
> this freedom seems to have been a necessary
> prerequisite to a deep knowledge of God. The
> devotion of a free, rational being is higher and
> more beautiful than that of an animal, re-
> markable though the love between humans
> and animals may be. But this human freedom
> involved the possibility of cruelty, unchastity,
> hatred and war—not only for the unbeliever,
> but for the believer also.[9]

If all choices led to the same result, then human
freedom would have no meaning. And if human

---

9. Wenham, *The Goodness of God*, p. 54.

freedom had no meaning, moral responsibility would be useless. There are two conditions under which all choices could be said to lead to the same result: if all consequences were good or if all consequences were bad. It is obvious, however, that an infinite God, who admitted the intrinsic value of moral responsibility, would have to create a world in which some actions would expose man to natural good and some would expose him to natural evil. Without unpredictable consequences, there would be no point in man's being free and no practical meaning at all to moral responsibility.

> The chief merit claimed for this solution is that it emphasizes what appears to be a fact of human experience; namely, that if natural evils are to be avoided, human choices must be made. If we are to eliminate the scourge of certain diseases, man must choose to conduct medical research and find the cures, if such exist. Since we do assume that many of the great evils that plague man can be eliminated by intelligent insight, the force of the solution is obvious. Only responsible choices can free mankind from the fetters of natural evil.[10]

According to some, this answer to the question of natural evil raises other problems which seem to cast a doubt on whether or not it really saves the character of God. Dr. Donald A. Wells lists the fol-

---

10. Wells, *God, Man and the Thinker*, pp. 142-43.

lowing problems in connection with this answer:
First, to say that natural evils must exist because
human responsibility requires them is to give a
psychological reason and not a logical one.
According to Dr. Wells, "This solution aims to show
that the motivation to choose presupposes good and
evil consequences to the alternative choices."[11]

Second, according to Dr. Wells, without different
consequences, there could be no incentive for man
to choose either one, good or evil.

Another difficulty with this answer to natural
evil is that it does not explain the number or the
seriousness of the natural evils which do exist.

> It is not merely the sheer number of natural
> evils, which appears out of all proportions to
> their function, but the seriousness of these
> evils. . . . hurricanes lay waste on an incredi-
> ble scale, a single frost can destroy all the ef-
> forts of a season, nature impales men, breaks
> them as if on the wheel, casts them down to
> be devoured by wild beasts, burns them to
> death, crushes them with stones like the first
> Christian martyr, starves them with hunger,
> freezes them with cold, poisons them with the
> quick and slow venom of her exhalations and
> has hundreds of hideous deaths in reserve.[12]

When God made a creature of freedom, he
opened the door to suffering. It could be no other

---

11. Ibid.
12. Ibid., pp. 143-44.

way. When God made the universe, he made it possible for man to use his freedom to find the good. But this inevitably included the possibility of evil and suffering. Why does man suffer? It is because he, or his ancestors, or his neighbors, or his friends have misused their freedom. In some way they have violated some of God's laws and have destroyed that which God wishes to be perfect and whole.

2. Natural evil is a potential by-product of laws that bring good results.

God has created a world that is governed by natural laws which, when they are in effect, benefit the world and man. The nature of the universe helps to explain some suffering and evil in the world. The whole universe is a system of law and order, a system in which everything is good and faithful. Scientific investigations made in one part of the world can be verified through the same kind of experiments in another. There is uniformity throughout the natural laws of the universe. There must be, or the world would not function properly. Principles true today must be true a year from today, if they indeed be principles of law and nature. Principles true in one part of the world must be true in another, or man would not know how to build a civilization.

This uniformity, this system of law and order, has much to do with man's suffering in the world. One example is fire. The natural laws of the universe, which God has created, include certain principles that enable man—if he uses the right elements and the right processes—to create fire. Today a man strikes a match, which is simply a cooperation of the laws of the universe. The same law that enables man to have fire for cooking his meals and heating his home also enables him to have fire that will burn houses and destroy people's lives. The law that made it possible to have fire for constructive purposes may be misused by man for destructive purposes. When man misuses the laws of the universe, suffering often results. F. R. Tennant says,

> it can be argued that the forth-comingness of our suffering is inevitably incidental to a moral order in a developing world. It issues ultimately out of what is inappropriately called metaphysical evil, or is a necessary outcome of a determinate cosmos of the particular kind that can sustain rational and moral life. The problem which it raises will therefore be solved if it can be maintained that no suffering which we experience is superfluous to the cosmos as a coherent system and a moral order, however excessive pain often may be as a means to the accomplishment of specific ends such as are attainable by discipline and chastening.[13]

---

13. Tennant, "The Problem of Evil," pp. 197-205.

Batsell B. Baxter says,

It is precisely because of the universal laws of nature that storms occasionally occur. God's plan of causing the sun to evaporate the oceans, of winds to carry the moisture in the form of clouds over the mainland, and of atmospheric conditions which cause rain creates the possibility of floods. As waters flow down the mountains and through the valleys, as the streams carry the torrents away, it is inevitable that occasionally there will be whirlpools with attendant danger to human life. The winds that normally purify the atmosphere occasionally cause a tornado.

Gravity can be cruel, when someone falls from a height and is crushed in the fall; but without gravity it would not be possible for the normal activities of life to go on. Similarly, fire is destructive on occasion, but without fire it would not be possible to cook man's food, nor to provide power for many of life's activities. Sunshine and rain are great blessings, though occasionally the sun causes droughts and the rain causes floods. It is necessary to look at the total picture. If we look at all of nature we find that it is very good indeed. The occasionally destructive aspects of nature are so few in comparison with its blessings that the verdict must be solidly in favor of God's system.[14]

14. Baxter, *I Believe Because* . . . , pp. 275-76.

Tennant says that

> the disadvantages which accrue from the de-
> terminateness and regularity of the physical
> world cannot be regarded either as absolute
> or as superfluous evils. They are not absolute
> evils because they are parts of an order which
> subserves the highest good in providing op-
> portunity for moral development. And they
> are not superfluous ills because they are the
> necessary outcome of that order.[15]

One of man's greatest achievements has been
the production of the automobile. But along with
its fine uses, there are also tragic misuses.
Similarly, steel, which makes great buildings possible, can also be used for guns and tanks, which destroy lives in war. The principles of nature, if properly used, result in good; but if used improperly,
they have within themselves the power for destruction. The only way a world can possibly work is for
the laws of nature and order to be constant and
faithful. When a man uses God's laws of nature as
he ought to use them, he prospers and is happy.
His well-being flourishes. But when he misuses
those laws, he suffers. The law of gravity is a wonderful and necessary thing, but its misuse can
bring tragedy, misfortune, and even death. So it is
with the other laws of the universe.

Some of these laws, however, involve necessary
by-products that seem to be evil. For example, the

---

15. Tennant, "The Problem of Evil."

survival of higher forms of life necessitates the death of lower forms of life. The bird eats the worm; the wild beast preys on lower forms of life; man kills animals to eat. Some people would refer to this as evil, but it is not evil. It is a necessary by-product of laws that bring good results and that God intended for the preservation of part of the creation.

The Atheist sees three problems with this explanation. First, it explains only certain kinds of evil, namely, those connected with animal pain. Secondly, a God who is described as omnipotent could have created a different kind of world without these evil by-products. And third, a God who is described as omnipotent could miraculously intervene in this kind of world to stop evil by-products without disturbing the overall moral fiber or upsetting these laws of nature.

Those who would argue for this would have God act in such a way

> that a wooden beam became soft as grass when it was used as a weapon, and the air refused to obey me if I attempted to set up in it the sound waves that carry lies or insults. But such a world would be one in which wrong actions were impossible, and in which, therefore, freedom of will would be void; nay, if the principle were carried out to its logical conclusion evil thoughts would be impossible.[16]

16. Lewis, *Problem of Pain*, p. 21.

This argument is given emphasis by the Atheist, who asserts that it "implies that God's hands are tied by the laws that He has established."[17]

3. The existence of natural evil helps man to contrast good with evil and causes man to recognize true values.

Many people believe that the world in which man lives would be monotonous and too boring to be endured if there were no contrasts found in it. Man has always been intrigued with opposites. Good is always found in conflict with evil. This, within itself, causes man to better appreciate the good. If man experienced only pleasure without having the contrasting pain, could he really say that he fully understood the pleasure that was there? An example often used is that the color red is learned and appreciated by its contrast with other colors. If everything in the world were red, one would not know what red really is. There are, however, three problems pointed out by the unbeliever. He says this view, at best, only explains some kinds of evils, such as physical evils and those that are connected with pain. He further states that much less pain would accomplish the same result; so why is there a seemingly insurmountable amount of pain in the world? Also, the appreciation of health and sanity does not necessarily mean a person must be sick or insane. If

---

17. Geisler, *Philosophy of Religion,* p. 383.

good depends on evil, then experience shows that a person cannot possibly know right without knowing or experiencing wrong.

Once again, J. L. Mackie objects that in the simple form this argument has little plausibility in providing an answer to the problem of evil. According to Mackie, this argument restricts the power of God, making God subject to causal law. A causal law says that to reach a certain end you must use a certain means. If God had to introduce evil as a means to good, then God is subject to certain causal laws.[18]

If this is true, it conflicts with the theist's ordinary view of what is meant by the term "omnipotent." If God is limited by natural law, Mackie argues, this conflicts with the view that causal laws are themselves made by God. If this be true, then the creation is more omnipotent than the omnipotent God that created it.[19]

The answer, then, that evil forms a necessary contrast with good is not entirely false. This does not, however, answer the problem of the great amount of disasters in the world or the gross inhumanities that occur.

4. The existence of natural evil is used to punish the wicked.

Another view is that natural calamities, such as sickness, earthquakes, tornadoes, and death are

18. Mackie, "Evil and Omnipotence," p. 285.
19. Ibid.

sent as a judgment from God on the wicked. "That man must not have been living right." "I wonder what he did so wrong that caused him to suffer such a tragedy?" "Why did God take my father from me?" Each of the preceding statements is directly related to the thought that suffering in this life is a result of divine punishment on a person for a specific sin committed by him.

This type of reasoning has been with man for a long time. Scripture relates an incident in the life of Christ when the disciples of Jesus asked if suffering were related directly to some wrongdoing. "As he went along, he saw a man blind from birth. His disciples asked him, 'Rabbi, who sinned, this man or his parents, that he was born blind?' 'Neither this man nor his parents sinned,' said Jesus." The reason for the man's blindness, says Christ, is "so that the work of God might be displayed in his life" (John 9:1-2—NIV). It is here asserted that some miseries and griefs are caused by something other than divine retribution.

The idea that suffering is retribution for sin is as old as man. The fall of Adam and Eve, the story of Cain and Abel, and many other incidents all stand as witness to the truthfulness of this suggested solution. When man disobeys God's will in life, he suffers.

While it is true that there is a large area of human grief that is a result of man's wrongdoing, there are some events of suffering that cannot be accounted for in that way. For instance, why do innocent people suffer and the wicked seem to prosper? Is suffering a sign that a person has done wrong? If not, then is it just for God to allow that person to suffer? Is there any value in suffering? If so, what is it? To answer these specific questions, it is important to first establish the fact that suffering often is retribution or a direct punishment for sin.

The Scripture states that righteous people will be rewarded by a blessing from God and unrighteousness will be punished by suffering.[20]

From the desert of Kedemoth I sent messengers to Sihon king of Heshbon offering peace and saying, "Let us pass through your country. We will stay on the main road; we will not turn aside to the right or to the left. Sell us food to eat and water to drink for their price in silver. Only let us pass through on foot—as the descendants of Esau, who live in Seir, and the Moabites, who live in Ar, did for us—until we cross the Jordan into the land the Lord our God is giving us." But Sihon king of Heshbon refused to let us pass through. For the Lord your God had made his spirit stubborn and his heart obstinate in order to give him into your hands, as he has now done. The Lord said to me, "See, I have begun to deliver Sihon and his country over to you. Now begin to conquer and possess his land." When Sihon and all his army came out to meet us in battle at Jahaz, the Lord our God delivered him over to

20. Cf. Deuteronomy 5:9, 11:17, 28:15-68.

*us and we struck him down, together with his
sons and his whole army. At that time we took
all his towns and completely destroyed them—
men, women and children. We left no sur-
vivors. But the livestock and the plunder from
the towns we had captured we carried off for
ourselves. From Aroer on the rim of the Arnon
Gorge, and from the town in the gorge, even as
far as Gilead, not one town was too strong for
us. The Lord our God gave us all of them. But
in accordance with the command of the Lord
our God, you did not encroach on any of the
land of the Ammonites, neither the land along
the course of the Jabbok nor that around the
towns in the hills. (Deuteronomy 2:26-37—
NIV)*

*After you have had children and grandchil-
dren and have lived in the land a long time—
if you then become corrupt and make any kind
of idol, doing evil in the eyes of the Lord your
God and provoking him to anger, I call heaven
and earth as witnesses against you this day
that you will quickly perish from the land that
you are crossing the Jordan to possess. You
will not live there long but will certainly be destroyed. The Lord will scatter you among the
peoples, and only a few of you will survive
among the nations to which the Lord will
drive you. There you will worship man-made
gods of wood and stone, which cannot see or
hear or eat or smell. (Deuteronomy 4:25-28—
NIV)*

One writer says, "Such an emphasis, obviously, highlights the righteous character of God and his sovereign purpose to establish justice among men. It is not to be taken lightly."[21]

John Wenham says that suffering is not only good but also necessary. He refers to it as beneficient retribution, which he states is a good feature in an ugly world. Dr. Wenham says the value of pain as a deterrent is rather obvious, but even more important in the world is the value of retribution to the individual for wrongdoing. "Fundamental to the Bible, from cover to cover, is the notion that God not only deters, but that he also punishes."[22]

It must be kept in mind, however, that this only helps in understanding the continued existence of evil in the world today. This in no way presents an explanation for the origin of evil.

It is true that society cannot function properly if there is no consequence for wrongdoing. When man does wrong, punishment is needed, if society is to exist and function properly. "A World of sinful creatures requires the punishment of natural evil in order that justice may prevail."[23] The punishment may be for sins committed either by the person publicly or secretly, or, according to some religious views, sins committed in a previous life. This prob-

---

21. Ferguson, "Problem of Evil and Suffering," p. 15.
22. Wenham, *The Goodness of God*, p. 58.
23. Wells, *God, Man, and the Thinker*, p. 145.

lem was dealt with specifically in the Bible from the book of Job. Objections to this can be divided into two parts. First of all, the view is contrary to biblical teaching from the book of Job. Job was a man who suffered and yet was innocent. Also, Jesus indicated that sin was not the reason for all suffering (Luke 13:4). This answer to natural evil does not explain the apparent unjust distribution of suffering, which includes suffering from innocent adults and children, and even babies.

The suggestion that suffering in this world can be explained by sins committed in a previous life has several problems. They are as follows:

> 1. Biblical theism denies the truth of the reincarnation theory: men have only one physical birth and death (Hebrews 9:27). 2. Jesus repudiated the view that a certain man was born blind because he had sinned in a previous existence (John 9:3). 3. It does not explain why God permitted the sin in the first incarnation. 4. It amounts to a systematic delusion of Christians (or other Theists) as to why God is punishing men.[24]

Now, in answer to the question raised earlier ("Why did God take my father from me?"), the following should be of assistance. (1) God does not directly take anyone. Someone might ask, "What of death as a result of judicial ruling?" No one would

---

24. Geisler, *Philosophy of Religion*, p. 383.

argue that death as a result of judicial killing is equal to murder.[25] To argue that it was would make God a murderer, and such is not true. Satan is the murderer. He murdered the entire human race, bringing death into the world, when he seduced Adam and Eve in the Garden of Eden. Death is in the world because of sin (Romans 3:23, 6:23; John 8:44; 1 Corinthians 15:20-26; James 1:13-15). But the fact that death occurs, even sometimes as a result of a great tragedy, does not mean that the person or persons involved are being punished for a sin or sins they have committed. (2) This thought that punishment is directly related to a person's sins is refuted by Jesus himself (Matthew 5:45; Luke 13:1-4; John 9:1-12; John 9:30-34). (3) This proposed solution that suffering is related to a person's sin does not account for all suffering. Even if it did account for all suffering, it would not account for the existence of moral evil (sin) itself.

But why does God allow the wicked to prosper and the righteous to suffer? One answer is that

> the righteous can be confirmed in true holiness only by trials and sufferings; because God will not allow even the little good which the wicked may do, to go unrewarded; and therefore, as He cannot reward in the next

---

25. Someone might easily bring up judicial killing at this point, as when God ordered the death of certain peoples and nations. Judicial judgments, however, are not to be referred to as the same thing as murder. For an excellent discussion on this, see Ronald A. Iwasko, "God of War," *Christianity for the Tough Minded*, edited by Montgomery, pp. 99-108.

world, He takes this means of allowing it to be rewarded in this world.[26]

5. The existence of natural evil serves as an example to others.

It is believed by some that natural evil shows as an example to others how a man can be steadfast and faithful to God, even while suffering persecution. This pattern of suffering while still remaining faithful to God is one that is admirable for those who would follow the creator of the world. Once again, Job is cited as an excellent example. In fact, as one reads the book of Job, he sees that Job is suffering to show how a righteous man can suffer wrongdoing and yet remain faithful because he knows that no matter what happens, God is in control.

The Atheist presents several problems in relation to this explanation. First, he says it would account for only a small amount of suffering. Secondly, it does not account for the mass disasters that are in the world. And third, not everybody is Job, and the purpose backfires when the sufferer renounces God rather than praises him. In other words, if it is true that natural disasters afflict an individual simply to cause him, in turn, to be an example to others, what happens to the purpose behind the natural evil when that person, rather than praising God, curses God and dies?

---

26. Deharbe's *Catechism*, translated from the German by Fander, p. 94, as cited by Crawford, *Genesis: Book of Beginnings*, Vol. II., p. 3.

6. The existence of natural evil serves as a warning to the wicked.

Man commits sin and as a result often suffers pain and punishment. This pain should serve as a warning to the wicked that they must answer to a higher power. "It is a kind of divine megaphone to arouse a morally sensitive world to God's purpose for their lives."[27] It is argued that pain serves the useful purpose of allowing God to express his feelings about man's wicked ways. This affliction is to cause man to return to God rather than go further away from him.

When natural evils occur in the world, they should cause man's inner nature to be stirred within him toward that which is religious and to reverence a higher power, rather than to sit idly by in a state of indifference. "Until the evil man finds evil unmistakably present in the form of pain, he is enclosed in illusion."[28] When man realizes the pain is there, he will choose one of two directions, turning to or away from God.

Some men do not take thought of God until they experience pain and suffering. Man is so busy with himself that he has no time for God. To think or speak of God is to be "interrupted" from the norm of life. Augustine said, "God wants to give us something, but cannot, because our hands are full—

---

27. Geisler, *Philosophy of Religion*, p. 384. See also Lewis, *Problem of Pain*, chap. 6.
28. Lewis, *Problem of Pain*, p. 83.

there's nowhere for him to put it."[29] Man uses God
only in cases of emergencies. Each man wants to
live to be "his own" and not be bothered by any outside sources. Using this reasoning, C. S. Lewis
pleads with men to consider the value of suffering
to serve as a warning for man to turn toward God.

> Let me implore the reader to try to believe, if
> only for the moment, that God, who made
> these deserving people, may really be right
> when He thinks that their modest prosperity
> and the happiness of their children are not
> enough to make them blessed: that all this
> must fall from them in the end, and that if
> they have not learned to know Him they will
> be wretched. And therefore, He troubles them,
> warning them in advance of an insufficiency
> that one day they will have to discover. The
> life to themselves and their families stands
> between them and the recognition of their
> need; He makes that life less sweet to them. I
> call this a Divine humility because it is a poor
> thing to strike our colours to God when the
> ship is going down under us; a poor thing to
> come to Him as a last resort, to offer up "our
> own" when it is no longer worth keeping. If
> God were proud He would hardly have us on
> such terms: but He is not proud, He stoops to
> conquer, He will have us even though we have
> shown that we prefer everything else to Him,
> and come to Him because there is "nothing
> better" now to be had.[30]

29. Ibid., p. 84.
30. Ibid., p. 85.

The Atheist, likewise, sees what he considers loopholes in this answer to physical evil. He says first of all that physical or natural suffering often, instead of causing men to turn to God, causes men to turn away from God. Also, the evils that are used need not be so deadly in order to invoke the awe of those who are aroused by them. Surely a God who is described as omnipotent has less deadly but equally effective methods of causing man to be stirred within his own heart towards that which is religious. Finally, the Atheist says that evil demonstrations, such as earthquakes and hurricanes, are still considered inconsistent with the nature of a God that is described as omnibenevolent. In other words, the goodness of God would be a lot more powerful and effective in turning men to God than the evil which exists in the world.

7. Natural evil is lost in ultimate harmony.

In this explanation evil is compared with a musical chord that, when heard by itself, may sound wrong, but when used in the context of the whole score of the music, is harmonious. So also, an event that is seen in isolation and from the perspective of the finite human mind might be viewed as evil, but when seen from the infinite perspective of God is really good. Therefore, the problem of natural evil disappears when viewed from the standpoint of God.

C. S. Lewis states:

> On the one hand, if God is wiser than we His
> judgment must differ from ours on many
> things, and not least on good and evil. What
> seems to us good may not therefore be good in
> His eyes, and what seems to us evil, may not
> be evil.[31]

As good as this may sound, it appears difficult to
explain. If God's judgment differs so drastically
from man's judgment, then man cannot be sure
that when he speaks he is being accurate in what
he says. For instance, suppose what man calls
"black" God calls "white." Man's judgment referring
to the colors black and white would be so far off
that it could not be said that man was even close to
being correct. Suppose man says God is good. If
man's judgment differs from God's to the degree
just mentioned, has man really succeeded in saying
anything about God?

There are some cases when man must look at
the long-run outcome of a situation. When this
happens, man can see that what at one time looked
as if it worked for our evil, did not do so. However,
it could be said this is true of everything, and if
there is no relationship between what we call good
and evil and what God calls good and evil, God has
not really communicated with us in his Word and
told us what is good and what is evil.

31. Ibid., p. 25.

The Atheist objects and says that this explanation makes God a deceiver, since what appears evil to man is not really evil in his eyes. And the so-called "higher morality" has no meaning to man, because it is completely different from man's concept of what morality really is. It requires that what man ordinarily calls wrong is right when God does it. This double standard of morality would seem unjust. Why, for example, is murder right simply because God does it to man in natural disasters?

8. Natural evil is a necessary part of the best possible world.

This answer to the problem of natural evil in effect says that one must consider the total picture of the world with all the good it involves, rather than looking at just the small insignificant happenings of evil. The world in which man lives is the best possible world God could have made. If he could have made it any better, he certainly would have done so. The world cannot be perfect; therefore, the world has a minimum amount of evil in it to produce for man a maximum amount of good.

G. W. Leibniz discusses this and places the argument in the form of a syllogism as follows:

> Whosoever does not choose the best course is lacking either in power, or knowledge, or goodness.

God did not choose the best course in creating the world.

Therefore, God was lacking in power, or knowledge, or goodness.[32]

Leibniz admits there is evil in the world, yet denies the minor premise of the syllogism. He says God made this world the best possible world in which man can live. The pain and suffering are seen as a small fragment for the good of the whole. His example is that a general in the army would prefer a small wound with a great victory over no victory to avoid the wound. To him, "An imperfection in the part may be required for a greater perfection of the whole."[33]

> I have followed therein the opinion of St. Augustine, who said a hundred times that God permitted evil in order to derive from it good, that is to say, a greater good; and Thomas Aquinas says ... that the permission of evil tends toward the good of the universe.[34]

Just as one piece in a carpet that is woven together might contain a flaw or mistake as it is viewed from one side, yet the essential part of the whole has so interwoven that mistake that it is not noticeable when viewed as a whole.

---

32. G. W. Leibniz, "Evil and the Best Possible World," as cited by Hick, *Classical and Contemporary Readings in the Philosophy of Religion.*

33. Ibid., p. 69.

34. Ibid.

There are a number of objections that the Atheist has for this explanation of natural evil. He says (1) an all-powerful God could have made a world without any evil in it. (2) A minimum amount of evil is incompatible with a God who is described as absolutely perfect. (3) Even granting that evil is a part of the total picture of good, still a better total picture could have been made for this world if there were no evil. Also, there is an unjust distribution of evil in the world. The Atheist says, "The Theistic God is like the old school master who punished the whole class because of what a few individuals did."[35]

This thought could be carried further with its implications. Not only could it be said that natural evil is a necessary part of the best possible world, but that natural evil is a necessary condition for achieving the best possible world. It is meant by this that without the existence of natural evil, the world could not be the "best possible world."

Natural evil is a necessary condition for achieving the best possible world.

This argument says that the present natural evils of this life will eventually, in the long run, lead to good. The expression is used, "All is well that ends well." Some have thought to explain this by referring to suffering as a means to higher good. It is believed that the reason God allowed suffering is

---

35. Geisler, *Philosophy of Religion*, p. 384.

because it causes man to rise to heroism, which probably would not be reached if the suffering did not exist. Pain, which often accompanies suffering, is viewed as a stimulus to activities that have made civilization and cultural achievements possible.

George Thomas says that

> recent philosophers have emphasized the limitations of this attempt to justify pain and suffering. Distinguishing between the "first order evil" of suffering and pain, on the one hand, and "second order evil" such as moral evil and "second order good" such as moral virtue on the other, J. L. Mackie criticizes the view that "first order evil" is a necessary condition of "second order good" and that its value in this respect outweighs the suffering it involves.[36]

This means pain and misery and disease are necessities that bring the noble virtues of courage and endurance and benevolence and other higher qualities of man's morality into existence.

The Atheist objects on several grounds: (1) It does not explain why God permitted in the first place those first-order evils. Could not God have achieved the same end without using such means? (2) The price in the long run is too high to pay. In other words, the end does not justify the means, when the means are evil. (3) Some long-run consequences are not good, but evil. Sometimes evil only

---

36. Thomas, *Philosophy and Religious Beliefs*, p. 237.

produces more evil. (4) How long is the long run? Either the person who believes in God does not know, or else he tells man the long run is when good appears; but that is just arguing in a circle. (5) Immortal bliss does not really compensate for evil suffered in this life. A person cannot be consoled when he is the victim of a tragedy by simply telling him that blessings will follow. What about the present suffering of that individual?

Natural evils that occur in life are disciplines.

One further thought is that natural evils that occur in life are disciplines that are necessary to produce spiritual beings for a better world. A world without tears could not produce charity or sympathy. A world without suffering could not understand relief from pain. Pressure causes the individual to rise to the top, and pain is the perfecting process whereby man is able to be molded by God into what God wants him to be. The Bible emphasizes the idea that suffering serves as a discipline.[37] Man grows in spiritual and moral qualities as he suffers. The emphasis is that suffering is, within itself, a message from God to man. As man suffers, he actually meets God with a deeper sense of fellowship, because when he is suffering he must come to God for help in that crisis. Suffering has the power to beautify and ennoble the character

---

37. Proverbs 3:11, 13:24, 15:5; Job 5:17, 33:19 ff., 36:13 ff.; 2 Corinthians 12:7-10; Romans 5:3-5; Hebrews 12:5-11.

and the spirit of the one who suffers. Some people feel that the love of God guarantees they will be able to have everything they wish; life will simply be a bed of roses untarnished and untainted by anything. This is unreasonable. God's love for man is never described in the Scripture as the soft, indulgent honoring of the child in the manner that sometimes is attributed to grandfathers. Rather, the figures of speech the Bible uses to convey the infinite love God has for man indicate discipline rather than license. God is pictured as a builder who cuts and places stones in such a way as to make a beautiful edifice. He is a shepherd who devotedly cares for, but also guides and restricts, his flock for their own safety. He is a father who disciplines and corrects every son whom he receives.

> *And you have forgotten that word of encouragement that addresses you as sons: "My son, do not make light of the Lord's discipline, and do not lose heart when he rebukes you, because the Lord disciplines those he loves, and he punishes everyone he accepts as a son." Endure hardship as discipline; God is treating you as sons. For what son is not disciplined by his father? If you are not disciplined (and everyone undergoes discipline), then you are illegitimate children and not true sons. Moreover, we have all had human fathers who disciplined us and we respected them for it. How much more should we submit to the Father of our spirits and live! Our fathers disciplined us*

for a little while as they thought best; but God disciplines us for our good, that we may share in his holiness. No discipline seems pleasant at the time, but painful. Later on, however, it produces a harvest of righteousness and peace for those who have been trained by it. Therefore, strengthen your feeble arms and weak knees. "Make level paths for your feet," so that the lame may not be disabled, but rather healed. (Hebrews 12:5-13—NIV)

A father who genuinely loves his child must from time to time cause that child to suffer through the administration of discipline, lest the child destroy himself and bring upon himself greater suffering by his own blunders. Loving care involves discipline. If God promised immunity from suffering to those who follow him, men would serve God only out of self-interest. As a kind of cosmic insurance policy, men would become followers of God. It would be foolish not to follow God, if to follow him meant that one would automatically be protected from illness, death, and disappointments of every kind. But this would defeat the real essence of religion. The earnest and genuine offering of worshipful love and devotion to God from man is a free response. If God offered immunity from suffering to all those who followed him, he would also rob them of the means of developing the beauty and strength of character for which all should strive in this lifetime. God does not promise his children that they will be immune to all suffering and evil. But he does promise, in Romans 8:28, "that to them that love God, all things work together for good, even to them that are called according to his purpose."

The Atheist criticizes by saying that character building does not apply to certain kinds of evil, such as insanity or brainwashing. At best, this can only account for small amounts of evil and would not include mass disasters or maiming of character. And the price that must be paid is too high. God could have produced spiritually significant beings without allowing physical evil as a necessary means to that end. If some good depends on evil, then man should not work to eliminate that evil, lest he be working against the greater good that can be accomplished by the presence of that evil.

Dr. Donald A. Wells says the two major problems with this answer to suffering are: (1) It asserts that without suffering there would be no high moral character in man. (2) The distribution of suffering appears unrelated to the need for disciplined character.[38]

Summary and Conclusion

To conclude the discussion of natural evil, it is noteworthy to mention that Dr. Elton Trueblood says that in the history of religious thought there are three main answers to the problem of natural evil. He lists them as follows:[39]

---

38. Wells, *God, Man and the Thinker,* p. 145.
39. Trueblood, *Philosophy of Religion,* pp. 253-56.

1. Personal life cannot develop in a stable environment. The question is not whether this is the best possible world, but whether this may be the only possible world. Natural disasters are inevitable in the universe.

2. Much suffering is, or can be, redemptive. It is true that the problem of evil is not answered completely by this, but it certainly lessens the force of the problem.

3. The third consideration is that of the life everlasting. "For I reckon that the sufferings of this present time are not worthy to be compared with the glory which shall be revealed to us-ward" (Romans 8:18). The argument, in logical form, looks like this:

> There is good reason to believe that God is just and that He is wholly just.
> But justice is never perfectly accomplished in this life.
> Therefore, if God is not to be defeated, there must be another life in which perfect justice denied here is fully achieved.[40]

These answers do not completely satisfy the problem of the origin or continued existence of natural evil. While it is true that the answers themselves have difficulties, they do, nonetheless, offer possibilities for an explanation to the problem. Each answer is an attempt to offer an explanation

---

40. Ibid. p. 256.

to either (1) the origin of natural evil, or (2) the continued existence of natural evil in the world.

For example, answers 1 and 2 seek to explain the origin of natural evil by showing that man misuses his freedom and, as a result of breaking God's natural laws of the universe, brings calamities upon himself and his fellowman. Answers 3 through 8 grant the existence of natural evil as a fact and seek to understand and explain how the continued existence of natural evil in the world can be used by God (1) to cause man to recognize true values, (2) to punish the wicked, (3) to serve as an example to man, or (4) to warn man of impending destruction because of his evil ways. It is significant to note that even granting the continued existence of natural evil, God does not allow natural evil to rule the universe in such a way that the creation could be referred to as bad. As explained in the last answer, natural evil is lost in the ultimate harmony of God's universe. One attempt to answer the problem that is rejected in this study is that natural evil is a necessary part of the best possible world. This is not true. Natural evil is the result of man's sinful misuse of God's world. God simply uses natural evil to accomplish his purposes in turning men back to him.

Each answer given contains a certain amount of merit. Perhaps no one answer, by itself, would suffice to some. Among the former answers given, there is one answer presented that has strengths biblically and logically. The strongest answer that can account for the problem of natural evil is the fact that when God created man, he gave man freedom of will. Man has misused this freedom and brought on himself and the world disasters that otherwise would not be here. Thus, both the origin and continued existence of natural evil are related to man's freedom of will. God's potential for man was good, but man disobeyed God and brought evil, pain, and suffering into the world. The answer of man's freedom of choice not only accounts for the natural evils of today, but also accounts for the origin of it in the world.

3

Why Do Bad Things Happen to Good People?

The Problem of Moral Evil

It is traditional to distinguish between natural evil and moral evil. Natural evil was discussed in the last chapter, now the task is to present an understanding of moral evil. The problem of moral evil is related to natural evil, but it raises difficulties unique to itself and therefore must be treated separately. Elton Trueblood says, "Moral evil is far more serious than natural evil and yet it is the more easily understood."[1]

---

1. Trueblood, *Philosophy of Religion*, p. 248.

The Problem Stated

The problem of moral evil is connected with man's freedom of choice. The problem may be stated thus: If God is good, then why did he create men who commit such moral evil and who bring misery on both themselves and others?

The problem has been stated as follows:

> Let us assume that God exists, is omnibenevolent (all-good), omniscient (all-knowing), and omnipotent (all-powerful). If He is omnibenevolent, it is often suggested, then He is willing to always prevent evil. If He is omniscient, He knows how to do so. If He is omnipotent, then He can do so. Hence, if God exists, then evil does not. But evil plainly does exist. So God does not.[2]

A formal statement of the problem is as follows:

1. Evil exists.
2. An omnipotent God could destroy evil.
3. A benevolent God would destroy evil.
4. Therefore, since evil is not destroyed, either—
   a. God is omnipotent but malevolent in some way, or
   b. God is benevolent but impotent in some way, or
   c. God is both malevolent and impotent, or
   d. There is no God at all.[3]

---

2. Yandell, *Basic Issues in the Philosophy of Religion*, p. 43.
3. Geisler, *Philosophy of Religion*, p. 349.

The Christian would disagree with a, b and c as describing the God of the Bible. Therefore, the conclusion would quite naturally be excluded as false. The only kind of God the Christian knows is one who is described as all-powerful and all-good. Norman Geisler says that

> if the theist wishes to back off from his insistence that God must be absolutely powerful and perfect (and, hence, forsake his theism), then some kind of finite God is the most he can conclude in view of the problem of evil.[4]

The Christian would respond to the premise that says a benevolent God would destroy evil by saying that God is destroying evil and will one day complete the job. This might offer an explanation for evil, but it leaves two problems unanswered. (1) Why did God allow evil to begin? (2) Where is the proof that God will eventually destroy evil?

Criticism by the atheist

In answer to the first question, one would reply that God allowed evil to enter the world through his creation, man. God created man with the freedom of choice. But if this is true, says the critic, then one must grant the following line of reasoning:

> 1. God made all that is in the world, including human freedom.

---

4. Ibid., p. 350.

2. Human freedom brought moral evil into the world.
3. Therefore, God is responsible for what brought moral evil into the world and therefore is responsible for moral evil.[5]

Response by the Christian

The Christian would object to the last part of the third premise by saying that God is responsible only for the possibility of evil's entering the world, but is not responsible for its actual existence. God is responsible only for acts he actually performs. God does not perform morally evil acts; man in his freedom does this. Therefore, God is not responsible when human beings perform morally evil acts.

The Traditional Defense

Man's freedom of will has been described as the traditional defense of God's righteousness, or "theodicy."[6] According to Hick, there are three stages to this type of defense.

First, there is the concept of God's omnipotence. By omnipotence it is not meant that God can do the logically impossible. Hick says:

> It is argued that God's all-power does not mean that he can do anything, if "anything" is held to include self-contradictions such as making a round square, or a horse that has

---

5. Ibid.
6. Hick, *Evil and the God of Love*, p. 301.

none of the characteristics of a horse, or an object whose surface is and is not red all over at the same time. The self-contradictory, or logically absurd, does not fall within the scope of God's omnipotence; for a self-contradiction, being a logically meaningless form of words, does not describe anything that might be either done or not done.[7]

God's omnipotence does not do away with the fact that some things are impossible for God. In relationship to moral impossibilities, it is impossible for God to lie. Because God is a moral being, he cannot lie. In relationship to intellectual thought, it is impossible for God to conceive the false as if it were true. In relationship to knowledge, it is impossible for God to know things that are not, as if they were. Or, in relationship to the physical, God cannot make a part equal to the whole.

This does not, however, mean that God is not omnipotent. It is just a fact that the things previously mentioned cannot be done. As Thomas Aquinas says, "it is more appropriate to say that such things cannot be done, than that God cannot do them."[8]

Second, there is a necessary connection between man's moral freedom and personality such that

> the idea of the creation of personal beings who are not free to choose wrongly as well as

---

7. Ibid.
8. As quoted by Hick, Ibid.

rightly is self-contradictory and therefore does not fall within the scope of the divine omnipotence.[9]

Man is not a mere puppet or automaton. He is capable of entering into a personal relationship with his creator. This being true, man must be endowed with complete freedom of choice. Freedom of choice is one characteristic that distinguishes personal life from nonpersonal life. Man must, therefore, be free to choose between right and wrong. This makes man a morally responsible agent with the power of moral choice.[10]

Free will is necessary if man is to glorify God. If God created man to his own glory, then the created order must be good to glorify a good God. What creature could satisfy a creator of such absolute goodness and love? Only a creature that is capable of the highest form of good or who is capable of evoking love from the creator and capable of loving the creator in return could satisfy such requirements. This necessitates free will. And free will makes evil possible. However, free will is also necessary in order to have love and goodness. A created thing could be admired and/or praised, but it could not evoke love.

A parallel relationship is that between a father and son. Would a father want a son who is a robot?

---

9. Ibid., p. 302.
10. Ibid.

This would hardly be acceptable. But granting free will to the son (thus making the son more than a robot) grants the possibility of complete rejection of the father by the son. Does this possibility keep the father from desiring the son? On the contrary, the freedom of the son to deny obedience and love to his father makes the obedience and love of the son for the father more precious.

Third, let it be granted that God is going to make persons, not robots or automatons, and that these persons are going to have freedom of will. Could God have made man so that he would always choose the right? Is it not possible for God to create man with a moral perfection that would enable him to overcome the temptation to sin? This means God would create a man whose nature would be perfect and the actions flowing from that nature would constitute a perfect response to that environment.[11] Hick says:

> It would therefore seem that an omnipotent deity creating *ex nihilo*, and determining solely by His own sovereign will both the nature of the beings whom He creates and the character of the environment in which He places them, could if He wishes produce perfect persons who, while free to sin and even perhaps tempted to sin, remain forever sinless.[12]

---

11. Ibid., p. 303.
12. Ibid.

Criticisms Presented

The defense based on freedom of will has met with strong opposition, three versions of which will be presented here, namely, those of J. L. Mackie, Antony Flew, and H. J. McCloskey.

Criticism by J. L. Mackie

J. L. Mackie questions the assumption that free will implies the possibility of moral evil. He says it should be that God could make man with free will, but in such a way that a man would always choose the good.

Mackie says the choice that God had was not between making innocent automatons and free-willed beings who would sometimes go wrong, but he also had the possibility of making beings who would act freely but always choose the right.[13]

Mackie suggests another difficulty in the idea that God can control man's will, but does not do so. He says God could control a man's will to the extent that man does right, and when he begins to choose wrong, God could intervene and stop him.[14]

He further argues that if God can do this but does not, how can he be wholly good? Some would say that when God allows a wrong free act and does not prevent that act, the act must not be wholly wrong. The freedom of the act then outweighs the wrongness of the act. If God took away

13. Mackie, "Evil and Omnipotence."
14. As cited by Thomas, *Philosophy and Religious Beliefs*, p. 245.

both the wrongness of the act and the freedom of the act, there would be not value at all.[15]

In answer to Mackie it should be noted that freedom that is limited in this way is really no freedom at all. If God were to leave men the free will to do right and were to intervene every time they began to act wrongly, this would be the same as making men such that they always freely choose the good. Or, it would be producing the same effect via providence instead of creation. In essence, there would actually be no real freedom at all. Freedom involves the possibility of doing the wrong as well as the right.

But, if God had made man such that he would always choose good over evil, then man's actions would be determined by God and there would be no free will.

God's refusal to intervene when man makes a wrong choice is not that "its freedom is a value that outweighs its wrongness," but this intervention by God would take away the possibility of both moral goodness and moral wrongness.

Criticism by Antony Flew

Antony Flew's view is similar to that of Mackie, but he has worked out its implications in more detail. Flew bases his argument on the principle that

---

15. For further information on his view see J. L. Mackie, "Evil and Omnipotence," cf. also Mackie, "Miracle of Theism" and the response by Plantinga in "Faith and Philosophy" 3.2 (1986): 109-134.

"acting freely" or "being free to choose" does not necessarily involve action that is uncaused or unpredictable.[16] With this as a base, he argues that it is not contradictory to say that God might have made people so that they always in fact *freely* choose the right.[17] Concentrated into a single question, it is asked, "If God made us, why did He not make us so that we should always want what is right?"[18]

The example used by Flew to support his case is the decision to marry a certain girl when there is no question of pressure socially, parentally, or ethically. Saying the man's choice to marry her was freely willed is not to say that his choice was uncaused or unpredicted, but knowing his own mind the man did what he did and rejected possible alternatives without any pressure to act this way. When a person says someone could have helped doing something, this does not mean the action was uncaused or unpredicted. It only means that if he had chosen to do otherwise, he would have had the freedom to do so. If this is true, however, then there is no contradiction in saying that an action was both free and could have been helped and was predictable and even foreknown.[19] With this view of freedom Flew says, "Omnipotence might have, could without contradiction be said to have, created

---

16. Thomas, *Philosophy and Religious Beliefs*, p. 245.
17. Flew, "Divine Omnipotence and Human Freedom," p. 149.
18. Hick, *Evil and the God of Love*, p. 304.
19. Thomas, *Philosophy and Religious Beliefs*, pp. 245-46.

people who would always as a matter of fact freely choose to do the right thing."[20]

In answer to Flew, George Thomas observes,

> According to this view, all men's acts are determined and their freedom consists only in the fact that their acts flow from their own volitions rather than being caused by external forces acting upon them.[21]

To this may be added the words of John Hick:

> The adequacy of Flew's definition of free will, as simply the absence of external constraint, can of course be questioned, and I shall in fact argue . . . that the Christian conception of the divine purpose for man requires as its postulates the stronger notion of free will as a capacity for choice whose outcome is in principle unpredictable.[22]

The basic criticism against Flew's argument is that he does not take into account that some things are impossible for God to do. Divine omnipotence, as has been stated earlier, is necessarily limited by that which is within itself impossible. God could not, therefore, make man with a free will and at the same time make him in such a way that he would always choose the right.

---

20. Flew, "Omnipotence and Freedom," p. 152.
21. Thomas, *Philosophy and Religious Beliefs*, p. 245.
22. Hick, *Evil and the God of Love*, p. 304.

Criticism by H. J. McCloskey

H. J. McCloskey argues three points.[23] First, he says there could be a lot less moral evil than actually occurs for man to exercise his free will. To him, God could have created man with a stronger inclination to do good and made the world "less conducive to the practice of evil."[24] There is a tendency to accept this type of reasoning. What man, at times of weakness and temptation, has not longed for a strength to help him do the good?

Secondly, McCloskey argues that the appeal to freedom of will can be justified only if the number of people who choose the good outweighs the number of people who choose the wrong.[25] This number must be "sufficient to outweigh the evilness of moral evil, the evilness of their eternal damnation, and the physical evil they cause to others."[26]

Third, he argues that moral values and the values of other goods must be compared. He then asks if free will values are so much more valuable than the next best alternative to justify the moral evil that is brought about by free will. His next best alternative is not a robot or automaton, but a man made such that he always chooses the good rather than evil.

In answer to McCloskey, the following is presented: (1) His first argument (there could be less

---

23. Thomas, *Philosophy and Religious Beliefs*, pp. 246-48.
24. Pike, *God and Evil*, p. 80.
25. Ibid., p. 81.
26. Ibid.

moral evil than actually occurs) implies that God has withheld from his creation the power to do good and has placed man in an environment unfavorable to it. This is not right and must be rejected. The Bible says that man is good and that the wrong that he does is not due to a bad environment, but rather results from his own choosing to do wrong. The emphasis of this chapter is that moral evil is the direct result of man's willful disobedience to God's laws and that God is not responsible for the wrong man commits.

(2) McCloskey's argument that the appeal to freedom of will can be justified only if the number of people who choose God outweighs the number of people who choose evil is not open to proof. There is no way of proving that those who attain to moral goodness outweigh the amount of moral and physical evil which results from the exercise of free will. Let it be supposed, for argument's sake, that what McCloskey is saying is correct. Grant that now there is more evil and suffering that is the result of moral evil than there has been good. What does it prove? It only shows that more men choose to do evil than choose to do good. This is what Jesus said in Matthew 7:13-14. Does this mean that because more men choose to do evil than choose to do good that God is responsible? Only the person who rejects man's freedom of will would argue such a case and hold God responsible for man's doing wrong.

(3) McCloskey then argues for the existence of a man made such that he always chooses the good. This discussion has already been covered and needs no further discussion at this point. It may simply be pointed out that it is not possible to take away free will from men and still describe man as a person; he would only be an automaton.

It is evident, therefore, that McCloskey does not give sufficient criticism to provide an answer to the problem he raises or offer an alternative to it. Therefore, an answer must be sought elsewhere.

A Proposed Solution

The problem of moral evil best finds its solution in man's freedom of choice. Moral evil is the result of man's choosing to disobey God. The best way to account for the existence of moral evil is described by the expression "freedom of choice," or free will. Free will means that man, within himself, has the power (ability) to decide for himself, without being forced, whether he will do what is right or do what is wrong.

With objections being given by the critics, as noted earlier, the question is asked if a Christian answer is possible or probable. What is the Christian's answer to the problem of moral evil? Is it the traditional answer of free will? Or are there other solutions to the problem? The problem of moral evil is heightened when a person considers that there are three alternatives that God could have chosen, but for some reason did not choose.

(1) Traditional theism admits that God could have elected not to create a world of any kind. God was free not to create. Creation flows from God's will and not from any necessity of His nature. (2) Further, theism acknowledges that God could have created an amoral world where there were no free creatures. Without freedom there would be no moral evil. (3) Finally, we admitted that God could have produced a moral world of free creatures who simply would never choose to sin.[27]

Norman Geisler discusses these under the heading, "Moral Evil: The Bind of the Hypothetical Alternatives."[28] It is within the third alternative listed above that there is a difficulty. How is it possible for God to create a world of free creatures who would never choose to do evil? Usually there are three answers given. (1) God could supernaturally intervene to prevent man's evil acts. (2) God could create only those beings he foreknew would only do good. (3) God could display his infinite power and glory to man in such a way as to cause man to be persuaded to always choose the good.[29]

Is God bound by alternatives? What is the answer to the problem, not only of the origin of moral evil, but to the problem of moral evil's continuance?

The answer to each question remains "free will." The origin of moral evil is found in man's fall in the

---

27. Geisler, *Philosophy of Religion*, p. 351.
28. Ibid.
29. Ibid., pp. 351-52.

Garden of Eden (Genesis 3). When Satan tempted man in the garden, it was in man's power "not to obey" God just as it was in his power "to obey" God. Man chose not to obey, and, therefore, sin entered the world.

The continued existence of moral evil remains answered by "free will." It is because man is a person, made in the image and likeness of God, that he enjoys "freedom of will." This is a freedom in every sense of the word: complete freedom to either obey or disobey. This is what makes man a person. Anything less would not be called a person.

There is no debate about the fact of the presence of moral evil in the world. The only question that forever remains asked in all ages is "Why?" The answer that is sufficient is that of the freedom of will given to man by God. This answer places the responsibility for wrongs in the world on man (where it properly belongs) and leaves the description of God's omnipotence and omnibenevolence unquestioned from the critic's objection via moral evil.

4

Why Me?

Divine Attributes and Human Suffering

The problem concerning good and evil in the life of every individual cannot be specifically answered. There is no way anyone can account for each incident that occurs in someone's life. There are, however, certain basic ideas or concepts to which a believer in God must hold. These are not to be taken in the form of laws, which either admit or claim attributes for God, but rather should be seen as guiding biblical principles that assist in our understanding something of the nature of God. They are as follows: (1) God is omnibenevolent; that is, God is all-good. Everything God seeks to do is only good and not evil. (2) God is omnipotent; that is, God is all-powerful and has the ability to accomplish his purposes.

According to one author, these two propositions are involved in a contradiction, and this presents a problem.

The problem is given in the following form: (1) God is all-powerful (omnipotent). (2) God is all-good (omnibenevolent). (3) Evil exists.

There seems to be a contradiction within these three propositions such that if any two of the propositions are held then the third proposition must be false. In other words, all three of the above listed propositions cannot be held at the same time without contradiction. And yet, all three of these propositions are held to be essential to theological thinking. The problem is one of obvious concern, not only to the theologian but to all Bible-believing people.[1]

The theist, however, does not believe there is a logical contradiction resulting from the two propositions as stated above.

As Wenham says,

> If the Bible's greatest difficulty has sometimes been made intolerable by exaggeration, other difficulties have been made insoluble by over-simplification. No solution can be right which either denies God's complete sovereignty over his creation, or his perfect goodness.[2]

---

1. This argument was presented in an article by J. L. Mackie, "Evil and Omnipotence." Mackie responded to a number of criticisms to this article in "Theism and Utopia," *Philosophy*, Vol. XXXVII (1962), pages 153-8.

2. Wenham, *The Goodness of God,* p.42.

It shall be the purpose of this section to discuss the two positions listed above.

God Is Omnibenevolent

It is here affirmed that God is infinitely good. To say that God is good and perfect in his goodness is to say that he would never do anything contrary to his nature as perfect goodness. God loves all that is good and hates evil. This belief, however, should not become a problem which would produce faulty reasoning in the life of the theist. The question is presented: If God is all-good, (1) why does he allow evil to exist, or (2) allowing that evil does exist, why does God not do something about it? Since there is evil in the world, is it really right for the theist to exclaim, "There is a God and this God is all-good"? Is the suffering man goes through good? Can the fact that babies are born blind and maimed be described as "good"? Is it good when an earthquake destroys an entire city? With these things happening, is it right for man to say God is good? Perhaps part of man's problem comes from a misunderstanding of the definition of the word "good" and from using it in reference to God.

Paul Little states,

> Perhaps the greatest test of faith for the Christian today is to believe that God is good. There is so much which, taken in isolation, suggests the contrary. Helmut Thielecke of Hamburg points that a fabric viewed through

a magnifying glass is clear in the middle and
blurred at the edges. But we know that the
edges are clear because of what we see in the
middle. Life, he says, is like that fabric. There
are many edges which are blurred, many
events and circumstances which we do not understand. But they are to be interpreted by
the clarity we see in the center—the cross of
Christ. We are not left to guess at the goodness of God from isolated bits of data. He has
clearly revealed his character and dramati-
cally demonstrated it to us in the cross. "He
that spared not his own son, but delivered
him up for us all, how shall he not, with him,
give us all things?" (Romans 8:32).[3]

C. S. Lewis says that often when man refers to
the goodness of God, he is referring exclusively to
God's lovingness; and in all probability, he is right.
Man today wants a God who is best described as a
God of love, who will overlook the wrong things
that man does. Man wants him simply to shrug his
shoulders when something evil is done and to say,
"It's all right, as long as man is contented in what
he is doing." Lewis continues,

We want, in fact, not so much a Father in
Heaven as a grandfather in Heaven—a senile
benevolence who, as they say, "liked to see
young people enjoying themselves" and whose
plan for the universe was simply that it might
be said at the end of each day, "A good time
was had by all." Not many people, I admit,

3. Little, *Know Why You Believe*, p. 157.

would formulate a theology in precisely those terms: but a conception not very different lurks at the back of many minds. I do not claim to be an exception: I should very much like to live in a universe which was governed on such lines. But since it is abundantly clear that I don't, and since I have reason to believe, nevertheless, that God is Love, I conclude that my conception of love needs correction.[4]

Believing that God is good convinces one that man, at his very best, is capable of being good, since he is made in the image and likeness of God. Man knows that goodness is better than evil, kindness better than cruelty, love better than lust, self-denial and sacrifice better than self-aggression and selfishness. If there is a God, his nature must contain and express all those things which are good. If his nature does not contain them, then that makes man, the creature, better than God. If this were true, man would despise God, who in that case would be just the opposite of good. It is true that

no Christian can allow lodgement in his mind of any dark speck upon the character of God. If God is good at all, and has implanted some sense of goodness in us, it is scarcely thinkable that there should be any trace of evil in him. Certainly no Bible writer imagines that God would or could do anything wrong.[5]

4. Lewis, *Problem of Pain*, p. 28.
5. Wenham, *The Goodness of God*, p.45.

Christ tells us that God is good (Matthew 19:17). Christ lived a perfect life, exemplifying all goodness, and told man that by looking at him man could know what God is like. Therefore, man has to keep many things, like disease and evil, in abeyance, awaiting further light. The Christian must also hold to the fact that it is impossible to believe God is evil, for to believe otherwise would be contrary to biblical revelation. On the other hand, if God is evil, then from where does goodness come? By making such a claim as this, the mystery of evil is replaced by a greater mystery of good.

Since God is goodness, love, mercy, and the very creator of all things, man can say it is up to God who will be blessed with good and who will be cursed with evil. It is by adhering to the Scriptures that one receives comfort from the words, "When I am weak, then am I strong" (2 Corinthians 12:10) or, "Thou wilt keep him in perfect peace, whose mind is stayed on thee; because he trusteth in thee" (Isaiah 26:3). There is nothing in the world that has the power to separate man from the love of God in Christ Jesus (Romans 8:35-39). Believing that God will keep man in his loving care causes man to find a God of goodness, love, and benevolence to all, a God who has the power and the ability to control life. God blesses all men because he is a God of love and a God of goodness.

The basis of God's interest in man is in the fact that man was created in the image of God (Genesis 1:26). Man is not a mere animal. God's chief concern has always been for man, whom he made in his image.

> Man is the crown of God's creation. He was made in the image and likeness of his creator and was given complete dominion over the earth (Genesis 1:26). "The heavens are the heavens of the Lord, but the earth hath he given to the children of men" (Psalms 115:16). Fallen man has lost that original dominion, but still possesses God's image (Genesis 9:6; James 3:9). Redeemed through Christ, God's incarnate son, believing men have already been moved positionally from the realm of a "little lower than angels" (Hebrews 2:7) to a realm "far above all principality, and power, and might, and dominion, and every name that is named" (Ephesians 1:21, 2:6). Glorified man will even judge angels (1 Corinthians 6:3).[6]

Peter says that God cares for man (1 Peter 5:7). Paul says that God loves man in spite of the fact that he is a weak and ungodly sinner (Romans 5:6-8). To those who love him, God has promised that all things will work together for their good (Romans 8:28). At the beginning of a passage that contains one of the greatest assurances for God's people, Paul says, "God is for us" (Romans 8:31). Before one can understand why good and evil exist and why suffering is found in the world, it is essential that he understand that God is for his people.

---

6. Whitcomb, *The Early Earth*, p.100.

To consider the relationship between the creature and the creator is, of course, to see a unique relationship, one that cannot be paralleled. God's love for man is seen over and over throughout Scripture. "In the beginning God created the heavens and the earth . . . And God saw everything that he had made, and, behold, it was very good" (Genesis 1:1, 31). Jehovah, the creator of the world, made this world a good world and crowned his creation with man, who was made to have fellowship with God and to love him in an intimate way. But man did not use his powers of choice and understanding properly; and, because of sin, he was cast out of the garden. From that time, man has been involved in a bitter struggle. The fall of man brings a breakdown of man's relationship to his fellow man and destruction into this society. All of this is pictured as the principle of evil at work in the world.

Christianity says God loves man. What does this mean? It means God loves man. He is not disinterested or indifferent, but he has a genuine concern for man's welfare. Man is the object of God's love. C. S. Lewis says such a relationship cannot be adequately expressed unless one uses analogies, and even then understanding might be useful but still inadequate. In expressing God's love for man, he lists the following: (1) The lowest type is the analogy of the artist for the artifact. In Jeremiah 18, God's love for man is pictured around the image of a potter and his clay. (2) Another analogy is the love of man for an animal. Men are God's people and pictured as his sheep in his pasture. (3) The next analogy, he says, is nobler and is seen in a picture of a father's love for his son. Jesus instructed that when a man prays he should say, "Our Father, who art in heaven" (Matthew 6:9). Lewis says,

> A father half apologetic for having brought his son into the world, afraid to restrain him lest he should create inhibitions or even to instruct him lest he should interfere with his independence of mind, is a most misleading symbol of the Divine Fatherhood.[7]

Finally, (4) there is the analogy between God's love for man as pictured in a man's love for a woman. This is a picture used in Scripture many times as Israel is depicted as God's wife.

Though these descriptions seem inadequate, they nevertheless express that God does love man and wishes only good to his creation. Lewis observes,

> When Christianity says that God loves man, it means that God loves man: not that he has some "disinterested," because really indifferent, concern for our welfare, but that, in awful and surprising truth, we are the objects of His love.[8]

---

7. Lewis, *Problem of Pain*, p. 32.
8. Ibid., p. 34.

In his words, God is not

> a senile benevolence that drowsily wishes you
> to be happy in your own way, not the cold phi-
> lanthropy of a conscientious magistrate, nor
> the care of a host who feels responsible for the
> comfort of his guests, but the consuming fire
> Himself, the Love that made the worlds per-
> sistent as the artists' love for his work and
> despotic as a man's love for a dog, provident
> and venerable as a father's love for a child,
> jealous, inexorable, exacting as love between
> the sexes.[9]

This deep genuine love God has for man is seen
very often in Scripture. Jesus said in Matthew
23:37-39,

> *"O Jerusalem, Jerusalem, you who kill the
> prophets and stone those sent to you, how often
> I have longed to gather your children together,
> as a hen gathers her chicks under her wings,
> but you were not willing. Look, your house is
> left to you desolate. For I tell you, you will not
> see me again until you say, 'Blessed is he who
> comes in the name of the Lord.'"*

A love such as this can only be appreciated and
probably never explained. To say that God loves
man and seeks for his highest good is correct. Only
when man tries to attach a trivial meaning to the
word "love" and looks on things as if he, not God,

---

9. Ibid., p. 35.

were the center, can the problem of reconciling human suffering with the love of God seem insoluble. Man was made that God might love him. Man is the object of God's love; and in response to that divine love, man is to love God in return. "We love because he first loved us" (1 John 4:19). An impressive statement of God's love is found in Romans 5 where it shows that Christ died for us when we were weak, ungodly, sinners and at enmity with God.

> This is the story of man and of God's dealing with man as seen in the front of the stage. Man was made good; he forfeited his goodness and his happiness by sin; God has taken steps to restore the perfection of human nature. Sin, with its attendant suffering, is a hideous evil allowed temporarily by a wise and loving God, but it is to be wholly overcome at the last day.[10]

A fundamental error is the failure of man to recognize God as creator and sovereign ruler of the universe. Millions of people literally refuse to entertain any serious thought about God. Morality is running rampant in immorality. Man refuses "to have God in his knowledge" (Romans 1:28). Still others, professing themselves to be wise, change the incorruptible God for a god of their own making. Others, like Eve, are deceived and regard God

---

10. Wenham, *The Goodness of God.*, p.47.

as standing in the way of their own progress and happiness. Therefore, instead of viewing God as one who is full of goodness for man, they view God as their enemy.

What man knows of God will profit him nothing unless his attitude is right toward God. Without the proper attitude concerning God, it is impossible to understand, even in a finite way, the problem of good and evil in the world. How can man comprehend good and evil unless he understands and displays the proper attitude concerning God, the giver and benefactor of all good existing in our world?

God Is Omnipotent

The theist believes that God made everything. All that God made is sustained by him. He knows everything, he is everywhere, and he has all power. He is described as the ruler of the universe. Man ascribes to God omnipotence, which means God has the power to do anything, since he is the creator, sustainer, and ruler of the universe.

The fact that God is the creator of the world makes necessary the inference that God is omnipotent. To think of God creating this vast world out of nothing and not having perfect knowledge and control over it is rather absurd. However, one contender states that

> he made a half-chaos of self-moving, brainless forces to be the bottom and the soil of his cre-

ation, out of which higher forms should arise. But then a semi-chaos, if it is to be itself, must be a field of limitless accident; and accident is by definition an uncalculated effect. It may be foreseen, provided against, discounted, or profited by; it cannot be intended or arranged. It would be meaningless to say that God himself planned the detail of a chaos, or of a semi-chaos either, in its chaotic aspect.[11]

The thought of God creating the world as a limitless accident is certainly not recorded in Scripture. There is no description in the Bible of God as a "celestial chess player, awaiting the unknown move, who by 'infinitive contrivance draws some good out of every cross accident.'"[12] In fact, the Bible says just the opposite. God knows every detail of his creation. Matthew 10:30 states that he knows the hairs of your head, and they are numbered. Psalm 147:4 says, "He determines the number of the stars, he gives to all of them their names." Nothing in the universe is an accident to God, for as stated in the Bible, God knows when one sparrow falls to the ground (Matthew 10:29). Everything happens according to the counsel of his will (Ephesians 1:11). God designed this world and made it perfect. The world is an orderly universe, a cosmos, not a chaos.

---

11. Farrer, *Love Almighty and Ills Unlimited,* p. 164.
12. Wenham, *The Goodness of God,* p. 43.

Many people feel that the biblical axiom that God rules the world has been allowed to recede into the background of man's thought. Man tries to avoid implicating God in evil and thus deprives God of his control over the world. For many people today who believe that God is in control, God's inactivity creates a great problem. Those who do not believe that God is in control say his passiveness suggests his intervention does not take place. This is not because God does not want to intervene, but because he cannot intervene. "If God wishes to control evil, but he cannot do so, we are reduced to Dualism, with a God of good waging inclusive war against a god of evil."[13]

The question yet remains, where is the answer for the individual who asks, "Why has this happened to me?" Or, "Why does God do this to me?" What comfort can be given to the ordinary man who has gone through suffering, anguish, and pain in the various circumstances of his life? John Wenham states that the intuition of the man who holds God responsible for what happens is sounder than that of the liberal theologian who wishes to exonerate God of all responsibility. He says,

> It is in fact cold comfort to say to a heartbroken person whose only child has been killed or whose husband has been fearfully injured: "This is not God's doing or God's will;

---

13. Ibid., p.44.

we live in a disordered world in which evil has been let loose; we must expect these things where sin reigns; but keep trusting God." Yet what meaningful trust is left if we cannot trust a child or a husband to him? How infinitely more comforting, more Biblical and more glorifying of God it is to cry with Amos in defiant faith, "if disaster falls . . . has not the Lord been at work.". . .

Furthermore, even if God could be absolved of all the responsibility for inactivity by his impotence, he could not be absolved of the responsibility for having allowed the situation to arise, for when he created the world he must have known the potentialities he was creating. Or, if he did not know what he was doing, we must add ignorance and folly to his impotence and inactivity.[14]

To say that God is not supreme ruler, sovereign and all-powerful in his rule, is to deny the God of Jesus Christ. Man cannot in any way blur the image of God as being the ruler, the judge, the all-loving and all-powerful creator of the universe. God is a personal God and is perfect in power, righteousness, wisdom, and love; and that image must be brought into focus. This God is the God with whom man has to do. He is the God in whom "we live, and move, and have our very being" (Acts 17:28).

---

14. Ibid., pp. 44-45.

This to some presents a problem:

> If God were good, He would wish to make His
> creatures perfectly happy, and if God were
> almighty, He would be able to do what He
> wished. But the creatures are not happy.
> Therefore, God either lacks goodness, or
> power, or both.[15]

Affirming the omnipotence of God is upholding
two views: (1) God can do what is possible to be
done, that is, he has the power to do anything.
"Omnipotence means 'power to do all, or everything.'"[16] (2) He will do only what is in harmony
with his absolute perfect nature. "The omnipotence
of God is his ability to do those things which are
normal functions of his power and which are in
harmony with his character."[17] This is the testi-
mony of Scripture which says, "With God all things
are possible" (Matthew 19:26). One thing that does
help in our understanding is to distinguish between what God permits or does not prevent from
being done to man and what he himself does to
man. God permits certain things to be done to man
about which we would not say he specifically inter-
vened and did to man. Charles Hodge says,

> The Lord God omnipotent reigneth, and doeth
> his pleasure among the armies of heaven and
> the inhabitants of the earth, is the tribute of

15. Lewis, *Problem of Pain,* p.14.
16. Ibid.
17. Weatherhead, *Why Do Men Suffer?* p. 26.

adoration which Scriptures everywhere present as the ground of confidence to his people. This is all we know, and all we need to know on the subject; and here we might rest satisfied, were it not for the vain attempts of theologians to reconcile these simple and sublime truths of the Bible with their philosophical speculations.[18]

Some, however, do not agree. According to Peter Bertocci, "The evidence indicates that God is not omnipotent."[19] Dr. Bertocci says there is too much superfluous evil in the world to say that God is omnipotent.

Would a good God who is omnipotent (or able to do all that is worth doing) not be able to create a better coordination of moral freedom, human ability, and environment than the actual situation seems to indicate? Do the facts about the human predicament in this world allow us to maintain the hypothesis that God is at the same time completely good in will and unlimited in power? Can we maintain that there is a Person who, in his wisdom and goodness, has seen fit to order the universe as it is?[20]

Such is the common complaint given by those who totally reject the absolute sovereign rule of

18. Hodge, *Systematic Theology*, Vol. I, pp.407-8.
19. Bertocci, *Introduction to the Philosophy of Religion*, p. 413.
20. Ibid.

God in his world. The unbeliever often likes to point out that if God is all-powerful and all-good, then he would do either this or that. In formula, it takes the following look:[21]

> 1. There are instances of innocent suffering.
> 2. An all-wise, all-powerful, all-good God would not allow innocent suffering.
> 3. Therefore, such a God does not exist.

When it is pointed out that such requested action is often impossible, the reaction is, "But I thought God is all-powerful and is able to do anything?" In reply it can be said that the word *impossible* implies a suppressed clause which generally begins with the word "unless." C. S. Lewis illustrates in this way:

> In ordinary usage the word impossible generally implies a suppressed clause beginning with the word unless. Thus it is impossible for me to see the street from where I sit writing at this moment; that is, it is impossible to see the street unless I go up to the top floor where I shall be high enough to overlook the intervening building. If I had broken my leg I should say "But it is impossible for me to go up to the top floor"—meaning, however, that it is impossible unless some friends turn up who will carry me. Now let us advance to a

---

21. Geisler, *Philosophy of Religion*, p. 127.

different plane of impossibility, by saying "It is, at any rate, impossible to see the street so long as I remain where I am and the intervening building remains where it is. Someone might add "unless the nature of space, or of vision, were different from what it is." I do not know what the best philosophers and scientists would say to this, but I should have to reply "I don't know whether space and vision could possibly have been of such a nature as you suggest." Now it is clear that the words could possibly here refer to some absolute kind of possibility or impossibility which is different from the relative possibilities and impossibilities we have been considering.[22]

This illustration is used to say that it is impossible for God to do certain things, but this does not represent a limitation of his power. Instead of saying God cannot do certain things, it would be better to say that such things cannot be done at all. If something

is self-contradictory it is absolutely impossible. The absolutely impossible may also be called the intrinsically impossible because it carries its impossibility within itself, instead of borrowing it from other impossibilities which in their turn depend upon others. It has no unless clause attached to it.[23]

22. Lewis, *Problem of Pain*, p. 15.
23. Ibid., pp. 15-16.

God's omnipotence applies to what can be done and to what is possible to accomplish, not to that which is impossible within itself. To demand that infinite power be able to do what is intrinsically impossible is to speak absurdly. God can do whatever is possible to be done; but because of his own nature, he will not even try to do what is impossible by definition.

For instance, some seem to delight in asking, "Is it possible for God to make a square triangle?" Or, "Can God make a stone so large that he cannot lift it?"

> Rather than saying that God cannot make a four-sided triangle, one would more accurately (or, perhaps more meaningfully) say (in light of the fact that the word "triangle" means a three-sided figure and cannot refer to any four-sided figure) that the making of four-sided triangles simply cannot be done.[24]

This is saying that some objections against God's power are not really objections at all. There is no success in even mentioning them in the first place. Lewis comments,

> You may attribute miracles to Him, but not nonsense. This is no limit to His power. If you choose to say, "God can give a creature free-will and at the same time withhold free-will from it," you have not succeeded in saying

---

24. Warren, *Have Atheists Proved There Is No God?* p. 28.

anything about God: meaningless combinations of words do not suddenly acquire meaning simply because we prefix to them the two other words, "God can."

Therefore, man can continue in his conviction that this world was created by God, and the existence of evil does not in any way disprove that God is in control and has full power over his creation.

5

What Can I Say?

Observations From a Christian

When one wrestles with the problem of evil, pain, and suffering, there is no easy, fully satisfying solution. It is not suggested that this presentation has answered all queries to the satisfaction of all minds.

The problem of evil, whether natural evil or moral evil, is two-fold. (1) There must be an answer for the *origin* of its existence. Where did it come from? How did it get here? Who is responsible for starting it? (2) There must be an answer for the "why" of its *continued* existence.

Philosophers and theologians who deal with the problem of evil and suffering fail to make a distinction in their answers between the two kinds of evil. Such a distinction is of great importance; but because this distinction is usually missing, some confusion has resulted.

Someone might ask, "Is this distinction really that important?" The answer is, "Yes." A person might properly answer the problem of the origin of evil by answering that evil came from Satan, from the free will of man, or both. But the question of why evil is allowed to *continue* still remains: Why does God, who is described as omnipotent and omnibenevolent, allow evil to continue? Why does God not put a stop to it?

When one believes in the existence of an omnipotent and omnibenevolent God, he finds himself in the position of having to answer the critics. Some proposed answers are not adequate. We will briefly mention a few of these inadequate answers and then present a view that we feel is quite adequate. These answers are presented from the viewpoint of the Christian; and it is to be presupposed that what is said comes from conviction that is guided by faith in a God who is omnipotent, omnibenevolent, and (important for our study) transcendent. It is hoped that these observations can help in some degree explain why suffering is in the world.

Some Inadequate Answers

One inadequate answer is that evil and suffering is just an illusion.[1] Much of this thinking is found

1. Trueblood, *Philosophy of Religion*, pp. 236-238; Geisler, *Philosophy of Religion*, pp. 311-12; Geisler, *Roots of Evil*, pp. 15-16.

in the eastern religions in their doctrine of monism. In the modern western world, this view is held by the Christian Scientists. It is difficult, however, if not impossible to accept this point of view. When a loved one has been diagnosed with some horrible disease and we witness the slow decay of their physical body, when we see their pain and agony, we are hard pressed to accept that what we see is an illusion. Norman Geisler asks the following questions: (1) If evil is an illusion, where did the illusion *originate*? (2) If evil is only an illusion, why does it *seem* so real? (3) Is there any *practical difference* between viewing pain or evil as illusion or viewing it as actual reality?[2] There is really no significant difference between someone actually suffering and someone thinking he is suffering. If a person thinks he is suffering, is that itself not a form of suffering?

Another inadequate answer is that suffering is the result of sin in a person's life. While this has some truth in it, it must also be rejected. Granted, there are many evidences that suffering is the result of man's own sin.[3] A man who drinks heavily or in some other way misuses his body will often eventually pay the price. The liar, cheater, and hypocrite will also inevitably suffer—sometimes in this life,

---

2. Geisler, *Roots of Evil,* p. 17.

3. Sexual sins often bring suffering upon the person who engages in them, and this example is used to point out that suffering is the result of man's wrong practices.

invariably in the life to come. But to say that this is an adequate response to human suffering is to answer too quickly. It may explain some suffering, but it does not explain all suffering. Think of innocent people who suffer. One significant example is found in the book of Job in the Old Testament. Job's three friends try to convince him that he is suffering because of some grievous, unconfessed sin. Job responds by saying, "I am innocent. I have done nothing to cause this to happen to me."[4]

A third inadequate response is that suffering exists because God cannot do anything to stop it.[5] This argument says that God does not want suffering to exist because he is all-loving, but that he is powerless to do anything about it. This is sometimes referred to as the finiteness of the God.[6] One difficulty of accepting this response is that it presents a picture of God that is totally foreign to the Scripture and to Christian belief. Man is finite, but God is infinite and not capable of being limited in the same way man is.

---

4. Other examples that the Lord dealt with are found in Luke 13:1-5 and John 9:1-3. The response that all suffering is the result of some sin is totally inadequate and therefore must be rejected.

5. Brightman, *A Philosophy of Religion*. Other representatives of this view would include John Stuart Mill and William James. For further reading on this you might want to consult the brief discussion in Trueblood's, *Philosophy of Religion*, pp. 240-43.

6. Carnell, *Philosophy of the Christian Religion*, p. 294. Dr. Carnell says that the concept of a finite God is a thought "which Scripture scores as untrue."

The Force of Our Defense: An Adequate Response[7]

Each of the previous responses are not adequate to answer the problem under consideration. We now turn to what is felt by many to be a quite adequate response to the problem of evil and suffering. That response is called the "Free Will Defense."[8] It is not supposed that the following response will adequately answer all the questions which might be raised.[9]

In brief form, the Free Will Defense is this: When God created man he created him with the freedom to choose. He could have created him with or without the capability of free action. If man had been created without this capability, God could have kept moral evil from ever entering the universe by making men automatons, so constituted to always choose good over evil. Instead, God created man with the freedom of choice. By doing this, he allowed for the possibility of sin by his creatures. Man did sin, and moral evil entered the universe.[10]

---

7. Hick, *Evil and the God of Love*, pp. 265ff; Plantinga, *God, Freedom and Evil*; and Peterson, *Evil and the Christian God*.

8. Plantinga, *God, Freedom and Evil*; et. al.

9. I am convinced that one of the main reasons it is so difficult to give an adequate response is that philosophers and theologians fail to make a proper distinction between (1) the origin of evil and (2) the continued existence of evil, as cited earlier in this chapter.

10. I believe that the biblical account of the Fall of Man and the consequent curse because of the fall, both on man and his world, are adequate to show that man himself is responsible for evil in the world, both moral and natural.

It is not God's fault, however, that evil is in the universe, rather it is man's fault. Since it is man's fault and not God's, the existence of moral evil is compatible with the existence of an omnipotent and omnibenevolent God because the inherent goodness of freedom with which man was first endowed outweighs any possible evil which free men might bring into the world. In addition, a world in which men freely choose good and evil is inherently better than one in which automatons do only the good. The presence of moral evil, therefore, does not disprove God's omnipotence. Rather, God is shown to be omnipotent by his ability to create free beings and by his confidence in creating beings who are genuinely free, even though they may use that freedom to revolt against him. According to Plantinga, a Free Will Defense is quite distinct from a Free Will Theodicy. A Free Will Theodicy, as offered by Augustine, seeks to discover what God's reason is for permitting evil. A Free Will Defense seeks (at the most) to say what God's reason might logically and possibly be in permitting evil. It basically defends the omnipotence and omnibenevolence of God against the charges of contradiction.[11] There are three stages in the Free Will Defense.

Stage One: The omnipotence of God. The first stage is based upon a view of the omnipotence of God. Divine omnipotence does not mean that God

---

11. Plantinga, *God, Freedom and Evil*, pp. 27-28.

can do anything, but only those things that in their doing and in their result are logically possible and do not contradict God's nature. God cannot make a four-sided triangle. Not because he is not omnipotent, but because, if the usual meaning of a triangle is retained, no four-sided figure can logically be called a triangle. In the same way, God cannot square a circle. At the heart of the Free Will Defense is the claim that it is possible that God could not have created a universe containing moral good without creating one containing the possibility of moral evil.[12] If it can be shown to be logically impossible for a perfect God to bring about the best of all possible worlds while prohibiting all possibility of evil, then the Free Will Defense is sustained.

Alvin Plantinga argues that God, though omnipotent, could not have actualized just any possible world he pleased.[13] He writes, "Among good states of affairs there are some that not even God can bring about without bringing about evil: those good, namely, that *entail* or *include* evil states of affairs."[14] For example, the amazing heroism that some people display would be impossible to achieve without evil being present in our world. In order for someone to display the grace of forgiveness, there must be someone to forgive who has commit-

---

12. Cf. John Hick's review of Plantinga's work in the revised edition of *Evil and the God of Love*, pp. 365-371.
13. Plantinga, *God, Freedom and Evil*, p. 34.
14. Ibid, p. 29.

ted some kind of evil. In order to understand what is meant when we say that man is good, goodness must be contrasted with other concepts such as temptation, cowardice, selfishness, etc. If man were created wholly good, there would be no clear understanding of these other concepts. There would be no meaningful moral goodness if there were no occasion to genuinely choose good as distinct from evil. The Free Will Defense, then, seeks to show that there is a certain kind of good that even God cannot bring about without permitting at least the very real possibility of choosing evil.

The presence of moral evil, therefore, does not disprove the omnipotence of God. A God who is able to create beings who are genuinely free to revolt against him is more powerful than a god who cannot do so. In order to bring about certain kinds of good in the world, genuine moral freedom must be permitted. A being who is unable to create genuinely free beings is thus unable to bring about the genuine good of creatures who freely choose right and freely choose to love and worship God. Such a god is not omnipotent.

Ronald Nash has restated Plantinga's argument in the following way:

> The whole purpose to the Free Will Defense is to show that the Christian's belief (1) "God is omnipotent, omniscient, and wholly good" is logically consistent with "Evil exists." The way to demonstrate this consistency is to

come up with one or more propositions that in conjunction with (1) will entail that evil exists. Utilizing Plantinga's reply to Mackie, we may formulate the Free Will Defense as follows:

1. God is omnipotent, omniscient, and wholly good.
2. It was not without [*sic.* Plantinga, "within"] God's power to create a world containing moral good without creating one containing moral evil.[15]
3. God created a world containing moral good.
4. Therefore, God created a world containing moral evil.
5. Therefore, evil exists.[16]

In the previous argument notice the following: Proposition (2) states that if God were to create a world with moral order, it must be created in such a way that both good and evil or genuine choices exist. Proposition (3) affirms that God created a world containing moral good and thus (4) follows as true. Moral evil, therefore, is the result of the world containing moral good, and therefore evil

---

15. This statement does not take into consideration the pre-fallen world. Prior to the fall, the world contained moral good with only the potential for moral evil. It is possible, therefore, for moral good to exist without moral evil because this is what the world was like prior to the Fall. But it must be granted that the potential for moral evil was present, or man was not genuinely free.

16. Nash, *Faith and Reason*, p. 193. Regarding (2) he writes in footnote 38, "My account here uses Plantinga's language but alters the numbers he assigns to the propositions." See *God, Freedom, and Evil*, pp. 54-55.

exists. But, the conclusion that evil exists is not incompatible with (1) "God is omnipotent, omnibenevolent, and wholly good."

Stage Two: Genuine personhood and freedom. The second stage of the Free Will Defense affirms a necessary connection between genuine personhood and real moral freedom.[17] "Genuine personhood" is defined by the fact that man is created in the image of God. The creation of truly personal beings, created in the image of God, who are not free to choose wrong as well as right is self-contradictory. A distinct and necessary element of human personality is real moral freedom to choose right and wrong. As it is impossible to have a four-sided triangle, it is also impossible to have a true, genuine person without freedom of choice. Instead of creating persons, God could have created some other kinds of beings with no freedom of choice; but since he created persons, it is necessary for them to have genuine moral freedom.

Since man is created in the image of God, he must have real freedom, that is, freedom of opposites. A restricted "freedom" may well exist, as with animals, but this cannot be true of man in the image of God. Evil must be a real possibility for man. If you put any restraint on the freedom of God, then you destroy the real sense of man being created in the image of God.[18]

---

17. Hick, *Evil and the God of Love*, (rev. ed.), p. 266.
18. Cf. Ramm, *The God Who Makes A Difference*, p. 129.

Stage Three: God and logical possibilities. The third stage of the Free Will Defense is where most of the discussion centers. It is usually accepted that God can do only those logically possible things that are non-contradictory and that are consistent with his nature. And, it is similarly accepted that God desired to make persons instead of automatons, and that they must be genuinely free. But could not God have so made persons that they would always freely choose to do right? Anthony Flew and J. L. Mackie say "yes" to this question, and in doing so, believe they have properly answered the Free Will Defense.[19] Flew defines a free action as one that is not externally compelled but which flows from the nature of the agent. Since this is so, acting freely is not incompatible with being caused to act a certain way. The bottom line of the argument is that man is "caused" to act the way he does by his own nature.

Several challenges have been made to this thesis. Stephen Davis argues that the proposition, "God created Adam such that Adam is free to choose either the good or the evil and such that Adam always chooses the good," is self-contradictory and describes a state of affairs that is logically impossible.[20] Criticism is also offered by John

19. Flew, "Divine Omnipotence and Human Freedom," pp. 144-169 and Mackie, "Evil and Omnipotence." See Hick, *Evil and the God of Love*, rev. ed., pp. 266-271 for a summary of their arguments.

20. Davis, "A Defense of the Free Will Defense," p. 339.

Hick,[21] Alvin Plantinga,[22] Thomas Warren,[23] and others.[24]

In spite of the criticism leveled against it, the Free Will Defense is still the most adequate and consistent defense of the Christian theodicy. Yes, there is evil in the world. It touches the lives of everyone. But the fact that evil is here and that it produces evil and suffering in our world is not sufficient reason to walk away from a belief in an omnipotent and omnibenevolent God. Properly stated we can say: "Evil really does exist but . . . it is not evil that evil exists."[25]

---

21. Hick, *Evil and the God of Love.*

22. Plantinga, *God, Freedom and Evil.*

23. Warren, *God and Evil: Does Judeo-Christian Theism Involve a Logical Contradiction?*

24. Ronald Nash mentions that the successful argumentation by Plantinga and others caused J. L. Mackie to acknowledge shortly before his death that the deductive "problem of evil does not, after all, show that the central doctrines of theism are logically inconsistent with each other." (J. L. Mackie, *The Miracle of Theism*, p. 154, as cited by Nash, *Faith and Reason*, p. 193.)

25. Warren, *God and Evil*, p. 277.

Appendix 1
Theodicy: The Problem of Evil and Suffering
An Outline Study

I. Philosophical Options: Dealing With The Nature of Evil[1]

A. Illusionism

This philosophy says that evil ceases to be a philosophic problem because all of material reality is considered an illusion. Eastern religions: doctrine of *monism* (Hinduism). Western World: Greek thinkers Parmenides and Zeno. Modern: Christian Scientists.

---

1. Geisler, *Roots of Evil,* p. 15ff.

B. Dualism

Dualism attempts to explain both good and evil. Found in Zoroastrianism and Manichaeism. Chief characteristic: it rejects any possibility of tracing the origins of good and evil to one and the same source. Modern forms: A. N. Whitehead and Charles Hartshorne. They incorporate God and the world into a bipolar God. One pole of God is the world (God's body) and the other pole is God's mind.

II. Philosophical Options: Dealing With the Nature and Character of God

A. Finitism

God is all-loving but not all-powerful and is therefore incapable of destroying evil.

B. Sadism

God is all-powerful and all-loving, thus he is generally unconcerned about destroying evil.

C. Impossiblism

God is all-powerful and all-loving, but it is either impossible for God to foresee evil, or impossible for him to destroy evil without going contrary to his own will.

D. Atheism

Evil exists but God does not, in fact, the presence of evil proves that God does not exist.

III. Theories of Evil[2]

A. Monism
Hinduism; evil is *maya* or *illusion*; such is the view of Christian Scientists.

B. Dualism
Zoroastrianism, opposed good and evil deities. A much less extreme dualism was propounded by Plato (*Timaeus*) and is found in various forms in the "finite deity doctrines" of Western philosophers such as J. S. Mill and Edgar Brightman.

C. Theism
Christianity is committed to a monotheistic doctrine of God as absolute in goodness and power and as the creator of the universe, *ex nihilo*.

IV. Major Historical Responses

A. Augustine (354-430 A.D.)
Two interlocking lines of thought.

1. Evil as a privation; i. e., a perversion of something good.
Evil has no independent existence, but is always parasitic upon good, which alone has substantial being.

Privatio boni: privation of good; derived from Plotinus. "Evil has no positive nature; but the loss

---

2. Hick, *Encyclopedia of Philosophy*, p. 130.

of good has received the name evil." "Being" is equated with goodness. Evil entered the universe through the culpable violations of free creatures, angels, and men. Their sin consisted, not in choosing positive evil, but in turning away from the higher good, namely God, to a lower good.

2. Aesthetic conception of evil; i.e., what appears to be evil

When seen in isolation or in a too-limited context, is a necessary element in a universe which, viewed as a totality, is wholly good.

Plato (*Timaeus*, 41 B.C.) through Arthur Lovejoy, "Principle of Plentitude." A universe which contains all varied potentialities of being are realized and which contains as many different kinds of entity as are possible is better than a universe which contains only the highest type of created beings. As an application, Augustine holds that the universe must contain mutable and corruptible creatures, compounded of being and non-being.

3. Augustine's influence

a. Thomas Aquinas, 13th Century

b. Luther and Calvin, 16th Century

c. G. W. Leibniz (1710)—"best of all possible worlds;" employed the two Augustinian themes. Best, not because it contains no evil, but because any other possible universe would contain more evil.

Summary of Augustinian Theodicy: The traditional Augustinian theodicy in respect to moral evil asserts that God created man with no sin in him and set him in a world devoid of evil. But man willfully misused his God-given freedom and fell into sin. Some men will be redeemed by God's grace, and others will be condemned to eternal punishment. In all this, God's goodness and justice alike are manifested.

This traditional theodicy has been criticized for its accounts of the origin and of the final disposition of moral evil (John Hick, *Encyclopedia of Philosophy*, pp. 137-138).

4. Criticism of Augustinian Theodicy

a. Origin of moral evil: Frederich Schleiermacher, 1830/31, says the notion of finitely perfect beings willfully falling into sin is self-contradictory and unintelligible. A truly perfect being, though free from sin, would in fact never do so. To attribute the origin of evil to the willful crime of a perfect being is thus to assert the sheer contradiction that evil has created itself *ex nihilo*.

b. Final disposition of moral evil: "If God desires to save all his human creatures, but is unable to do so, he is limited in power. If, on the other hand, he does not desire the salvation of all, but has created some for damnation, he is limited in goodness. In either case, the doctrine of eternal damnation stands as an obstacle in the way of Christian Theodicy" (John Hick, *Encyclopedia of Philosophy*, p. 138).

Augustinian Theodicy: The Augustinian type of theodicy teaches that everything was created out of nothing by a perfectly good God and was therefore created good. But angels and then man chose to concentrate on themselves instead of God, and, being lifted up by pride, sought to enjoy their own power rather than that of God. This abuse of freedom plunged the universe and the human race into sin. There is evil in the world, therefore, but it has no positive nature; it is a privation of good. Some men are redeemed from evil by God's grace, while others will be condemned to hell eternally. God is not thwarted in his purpose for the universe, however, because what appears in isolation to be positively evil is in reality part of a wholly good universe in which the infinite creativity of God is expressed.

B. Irenaeus (c. 120-200 A.D.)

1. Prior to Augustine

2. Among the Greek-speaking fathers

3. Regarded the Pre-Fall Adam as more like a child than a mature, responsible adult

a. Adam was made imperfect and free to become "good."

b. Adam evolved into the "image" of God (i.e., as personal) yet at an "epistemic distance" from God. Man had to be brought into a "likeness" of God (i.e., morally perfect).

c. The Fall, therefore, is seen as a delaying and complicating factor in the development of human race; was virtually inevitable in human evolution.

d. Human beings universally are sinful, but do not *inherit* guilt or sinfulness.

e. Life's trials are a divinely-appointed environment for human development and perfection.

f. Eschatological emphasis—perfection of *all* human beings continues far beyond this life. The resultant future good will be so great as to render acceptable all previous evils.

C. Contrast: Augustinian & Irenaean Theodicies

1. Augustine: to relieve the creator of responsibility of evil by positing evil to human freedom willfully misused.

Irenaeus: accepts God's ultimate omniresponsibility and seeks to show for what good and justifying reason he has created a universe in which evil was inevitable.

2. *Augustine:* embodies philosophy of evil as non-being with Platonic accompaniment of the principle of Plentitude; conception of great chain of being and the aesthetic vision of the perfection of the universe as a complete harmony.

Irenaeus: Purely theological in character; not committed to any philosophical frame work.

3. *Augustine:* sees God's relation to his creation in non-personal terms. Man created as a part of a hierarchy of forms of existence which would be incomplete without him, and existence of moral evil is harmonized within this perfect whole by the balancing effect of just punishment.

Irenaeus: man created for fellowship with his maker and is valued by the personal divine love as an end in himself. The world exists to be an environment for man's life, and its imperfections are integral to its fitness as a place of "soul making."

4. *Augustine:* looks to the past; fall of angels and men are the explanation of evil in universe.

Irenaeus: eschatological; justification for existence of evil is in an infinite good which God is bringing out of the temporal process.

5. *Augustine:* fall—central role; original righteousness and perfect world.

Irenaeus: fall not denied, but less important; original righteousness and perfect world are rejected.

6. *Augustine:* points to a final division of man: saved and unsaved.

Irenaeus: doctrine of eternal hell renders Christianity impossible.

D. Agreements: Augustinian & Irenaean Theodicies

1. Aesthetic concept of perfection of the universe in Augustine has its equivalent in Irenaeus eschatological perfection of creation.

2. Both acknowledge God's ultimate responsibility for evil.

3. "O Felix Culpa"—Theme common to both.

4. Both acknowledge logical limitations upon divine omnipotence (not a real restriction in God's power).

5. Augustine affirms and Irenaeus (at least) does not deny the reality of a personal devil and a community of evil powers.

6. A valuation (positive) of the world.

Appendix 2

Foreword to First Edition

by
James D. Bales

There are times in the lives of all of us when the problems of moral and of physical evil painfully stab us into asking "Why?" It has long been viewed as the basic objection to the existence of Almighty God who is also the God of love. There are some who want God to remove the very possibility of human conflict from this world. They do not seem to realize that this would mean the removal of man himself. There is either some freedom or no freedom at all. Without any freedom man is no longer man. But as long as there is freedom to choose there is freedom to consciously or unconsciously choose that which is wrong. And since choices have consequences, a person's choice for good or for evil will have an impact on others unless God places each free being in an isolation cell where no one can be influenced by either the good or the evil done by another person. What sort of freedom would it be to go through life imprisoned in solitary confinement?

Myers has fairly and forcefully presented the case which the atheists have formulated in order to use the problem of evil to deny the existence of God. Among other things, it seems to me that the atheists have failed to take into consideration at least the following. *First*, if atheism is right, there is no problem of evil or fact of good. To deny the existence of God is to deny the existence of evil. If there is no God, if man is just a mechanism, just matter in motion, one can say that some things are hot or cold, that some are pleasant or unpleasant, that some things feel good and some do not feel good, but one could not say that anything is evil. Without God there can be no moral law and no moral or immoral man. To say that something is evil is to say that good exists. One must expressly state or clearly imply the existence of the standard of good in order to say that anything is evil. How can the atheist explain the existence of good in a material universe which has no room for a non-material realm of morality? He cannot even say that physical evil is evil; he can only say some things are painful. In a nonmoral universe, things are whatever they are and one cannot apply a moral standard and say that they ought to be different, or that even if they were different that one was a moral situation and the other was not. The atheist, when consistent, must say that evil does not exist. The only logical ground on which he can utilize the argument is by saying it is an *argumentum ad hominem*. In other words, he would have to say that he does not believe that evil or good exists, but since we believe they exist, we must harmonize our belief in the existence of evil with belief in the existence of God, who is good and all-powerful. But as for himself, the atheist must say there is neither good nor evil. Once he accepts the reality of evil he must accept the reality of good. Atheism cannot solve the problem of good—and in their world view it is a problem—and hold to materialism. The problem of good should lead him to realize the existence of the moral realm and therefore to the conclusion that materialism is a false philosophy of life, for it has no room for the reality of morality. I have argued in some detail for the reality of the moral realm in my book on *Communism and the Reality of Moral Law*.

Second, atheists magnify the problem of evil, which is big enough as it is, by failing to realize that when one has experienced as much moral and physical evil as one individual can experience, he has experienced the greatest amount which can be experienced. The sufferings of many people leave on us the impression that somehow the degree of suffering has been increased because three people suffer instead of one. Although an individual may suffer because of the sufferings of another, each does his own suffering and when each suffers the total amount that an individual can suffer, it does not mean that there is a third person who is suffering the total amount the others suffer. When one suffers as much pain as can be suffered from a toothache, the suffering of another from a toothache does not mean that the total suffering is doubled because two people have a toothache. If everyone in the world suffers from a toothache, it does not mean that there is one composite person called humanity whose suffering is the total amount suffered by every individual. You do not add up suffering so that an abstract man, symbolizing all men, suffers the total amount that each individual suffers. This does not do away with the problem of suffering, but it does help put it in its true perspective. We are individuals on whom other individuals may have an impact, but it is as individuals, and not as a mass called humanity, that each experiences either the good or the evil.

Third, the atheist thinks that he has brought up an intellectual difficulty and advanced reasonable arguments against the existence of God. However, unless the atheist abandons materialism, which is inherent in atheism, he cannot claim that any position is reasonable or that he is being intelligent and we are not. If atheism is true, matter in motion is the sole reality, and he who says "I think" is saying the same thing as one who says "I itch." In both cases they are describing a physical sensation physically produced and one cannot say that one sensation is the reasonable one and another is not. Consistent atheism strips man of reason and says that he thinks as he thinks because of internal and external physical pressures. There are no other pressures or movements, for all that is, is physical. Although the problem of evil may raise intellectual and moral questions for the theist, who believes there is some freedom including some freedom to think, the atheist cannot claim that he is making out a reasonable case against theism. He is mechanically sounding off what matter makes him say but whether it constitutes any insight into reality he could never know.

Fourth, atheists overlook the fact that they have not really solved the problem of pain and evil in their own lives by denying God. They have denied thereby that there is any moral evil or physical evil and have said that man's case is hopeless. Once they deny God, to whom can they go to help them with life's problems and perplexities? There is no one to whom they can turn who can furnish them with meaning for life. Why let the problem of evil turn them to utter futility? Why face evil without God's help? Because one does not have all the light he might like to have, should he turn off the light which he does have and plunge himself into total darkness? To do so is not an act of reason and destroys all ground for any significant hope in life. Atheists ought to realize that although the Christian cannot answer every question or every problem, he can at least face these problems with God and therefore with real hope.

I commend brother Myers' book as a serious and helpful study of the problem of evil. It will without doubt help some Christians as they face the problem of evil in their own lives and in the lives of others.

J. D. Bales
Searcy, Arkansas
September 22, 1977

Bibliography

Abernathy, G. L. and Langford, T. A. *Philosophy of Religion*. New York: The MacMillan Company, 1962.

Allen, Diogenes. *The Traces of God: In a Frequently Hostile World*. Cambridge, MA: Cowley Publications, 1981.

Augustine, St. "The City of God," Vol. XIII of *Great Books of the Western World,* translated by Marcus Dods, 54 vols. Chicago: Encyclopedia Britannica, Inc., 1955.

—"The Confessions," Vol. I of *Great Books of the Western World*, translated by Edward B. Pusey, 54 vols. Chicago: Encyclopedia Britannica Inc., 1955.

Bales, James D. *The Biblical Doctrine of God*. West Monroe, LA: Central Printers and Publishers, 1968.

Bassinger, Paul. *An Outline of Confessions of St. Augustine*. Boston: Student Outlines Company, n.d.

Baxter, Batsell Barrett. *I Believe Because . . .* Grand Rapids: Baker Book House, 1971.

Black, Hubert. *Good God! Cry or Credo?* New York Abingdon Press, 1966.

Bertocci, Peter Antony. *Introduction to the Philosophy of Religion*. New York: Prentice-Hall, Inc., 1952.

Brightman, Edgar S. *A Philosophy of Religion.* New York: Prentice-Hall, Inc., 1940.

Buttrick, George Arthur. *God, Pain and Evil.* New York: Abingdon Press, Inc., 1966.

Carnell, Edward J. *An Introduction to Christian Apologetics.* Grand Rapids: Wm. B. Eerdmans Publishing Company, 1948.

—*A Philosophy of the Christian Religion.* Grand Rapids: Wm. B. Eerdmans Publishing Company, 1970.

Carson, D. A. *How Long, O Lord?* Grand Rapids: Baker Book House, 1990.

Clark, George H. *Religion, Reason and Revelation.* Philadelphia: Presbyterian and Reformed Publishing Company, 1961.

Clark, Robert E. D. *The Universe . . . Plan or Accident?* Philadelphia: Muhlenburg Press, 1961.

Cottrell, Jack W. *What The Bible Says About God the Ruler.* Joplin: College Press, 1984.

Crawford, C. C. *Genesis: The Book of Beginnings,* Four Volumes. Joplin, MO: College Press, 1968.

David, Stephen T., editor, *Encountering Evil: Live Options in Theodicy.* Atlanta: John Knox Press, 1981.

Davis, William H. *Philosophy of Religion.* Abilene, Texas: Biblical Research Press, 1969.

Demos, Raphael. The Philosophy of Plato. NY: Charles Scribner's Sons, 1939; Reprint, NY: Octagon Books, Inc., 1966.

Erickson, Millard J. *Christian Theology, Vol. 1*. Grand Rapids: Baker Book House, 1983.

Evely, Louis, *Suffering*. New York: Herder and Herder, 1967.

Fairbairn, A. M. *The Philosophy of the Christian Religion*. London: Hodder and Stoughton, n.d.

Farrer, Austin. *Love Almighty and Ills Unlimited*. London: Collins, 1962.

Feinberg, John. *Theologies and Evil*. Washington, D. C.: University Press of America, 1979.

Ferguson, Milton. "The Problem of Evil and Suffering," *Southwestern Journal of Theology*, XII, (April, 1963).

Finegan, Jack. *Beginnings in Theology*. New York: Association Press, 1956.

Flew, Antony and MacIntyre, Alasdair, editors. *New Essays in Philosophical Theology*. New York: The MacMillan Company, 1963.

Galligan, Michael. *God and Evil*. New York: Paulist, 1976.

Geisler, Norman. *The Roots of Evil*. Grand Rapids: Zondervan, 1978.

—*Philosophy of Religion*. Grand Rapids: Zondervan Publishing Company, 1974.

Geisler, Norman and Ron Brooks. *When Skeptics Ask*. Wheaton: Victor Books, 1990.

Griffin, David Ray. *God, Power, and Evil: A Process Theodicy*. Philadelphia: Westminster, 1876.

Hafeman, Scott J. *Suffering and the Spirit: An Exegetical Study of 2 Corinthians 2:14-3:3 with the Context of the Corinthian Correspondence,*

WUNT 19. Tubingen: J. C. B. Mohr [Paul Siebeck], 1986.

Hall, Douglas John. *God and Human Suffering: An Exercise in the Theology of the Cross.* Minneapolis: Augsburg Publishing House, 1986.

Harkness, Georgia. *Conflicts in Religious Thought.* New York: Harper & Brothers, 1929.

Hauerwas, Stanley. *Naming the Silences: God, Medicine, and the Problem of Suffering.* Grand Rapids: Eerdmans, 1990.

Hebblethwaite, Brian. *Evil, Suffering and Religion.* New York: Hawthorn, 1976.

Henry, Carl F. H., editor. *Baker's Dictionary of Christian Ethics.* Grand Rapids: Baker Book House, 1973.

Hick, John. *Classical and Contemporary Readings in the Philosophy of Religion.* Englewood Cliffs, NJ: Prentice-Hall, Inc., 1964.

Hick, John. *Evil and the God of Love.* New York: Harper & Row, Publishers, 1966.

Hick, John. *Philosophy of Religion.* Englewood Cliffs, NJ: Prentice-Hall, Inc., 1973.

Hodge, Charles, *Systematic Theology,* Three Volumes. Grand Rapids: Wm. B. Eerdmans Publishing Company, reprinted 1973.

Howard, David M. *How come, God?* Philadelphia: A. J. Holman Company, 1972.

Joad, C. E. M. *God and Evil.* Harper & Brothers Publishers, 1943.

Knudson, Albert C. *Basic Issues in Christian Thought*. New York: Abingdon-Cokesbury Press, n.d.

Kushner, Harold. *When Bad Things Happen To Good People*. New York: Shocken, 1981.

Lewis, C. S. *God in the Dock*. Walter Hooper, editor. Grand Rapids: Wm. B. Eerdmans Publishing Company, 1972.

—*The Problem of Pain*. New York: The MacMillan Company, 1948.

Little, Paul E. *Know Why You Believe*. Wheaton, IL: Scripture Press Publications, Inc., 1967.

Lockyer, Herbert. *All the Doctrines of the Bible*. Grand Rapids: Zondervan Publishing Company, 1973.

Lowbar, James William. *World-Wide Problems or Macrocosmos*. Cincinnati: the Standard Publishing Company, 1923.

MacGregor, Geddes. *Introduction to Religious Philosophy*. Boston: Houghton Mifflin Company, 1959.

—*Philosophical Issues in Religious Thought*. Boston: Houghton Mifflin Company, 1973.

MacIntosh, Douglas C. *The Reasonableness of Christianity*. New York: Charles Scribner's sons, 1929.

Mackie, J. L. "Evil and Omnipotence", *MIND*, Vol. 64, No. 254, 1955.

—*The Miracle of Theism*. Oxford: Clarendon Press, 1982.

Maritian, Jacques. *God and the Permission of Evil,* translated by Joseph W. Evans. Milwaukee: The Bruce Publishing Company, 1966.

Matson, T. B. *Suffering: A Personal Perspective.* Nashville: Broadman Press, 1967.

Mavrodes, George I. *The Rationality of Belief in God.* Englewood Cliffs, NJ: Prentice-Hall, Inc., 1970.

Mavrodes, George I. and Hackett, Stuart C. *Problems and Perspectives in the Philosophy of Religion.* Boston: Allyn & Bacon, 1969.

McClintock, John and Strong, James. *Cyclopedia of Biblical, Theological and Ecclesiastical Literature,* Twelve Volumes. Grand Rapids: Baker Book House, reprinted 1970.

Miller, Ed L. *God and Reason.* New York: The MacMillan Company, 1972.

Monser, J. W. *An Encyclopedia on the Evidences; or, Masterpieces of Many Minds.* Grand Rapids: Baker Book House, reprinted 1961.

Montgomery, John Warwick, editor. *Christianity for the Tough Minded.* Minneapolis: Bethany Fellowship, Inc., 1973.

Nash, Ronald H. *Faith and Reason.* Grand Rapids: Zondervan, 1988.

Nevius, Warren N. *Religion as Experience and Truth.* Philadelphia: The Westminster Press, 1941.

Oates, Wayne E. *The Revelation of God in Human Suffering.* Philadelphia: The Westminster Press, 1959.

Orr, James. *The Christian View of God and the World*. Grand Rapids: Wm. B. Eerdmans Publishing company, 1948.

Phillips, W. Gary and William E. Brown. *Making Sense of Your World*. Chicago: Moody Press, 1991.

Pike, Nelson, editor. *God and Evil*. Englewood Cliffs, N. J.: Prentice-Hall, Inc., 1964.

Plantinga, Alvin. *God, Freedom, and Evil*. Grand Rapids: Eerdmans, 1977.

Plantinga, Theodore. *Learning to Live with Evil*. Grand Rapids: Eerdmans, 1982.

Ramm, Bernard. *The God Who Makes the Difference*. Waco: Word, 1972.

Reichenback, Bruce R. *Evil and a Good God*. New York: Fordham University Press, 1982.

Ridenour, Fritz, editor. *Who Says God Created* . . . . Glendale, CA: Gospel Light Publications, 1971.

Roberts, Alexander and Donaldson, James, editors. Lactantius, "A Treatise on the Anger of God," *The Ante-Nicene Fathers,* Ten Volumes. Grand Rapids: Wm. B. Eerdmans Publishing company, 1951 reprint.

Robinson, H. Wheeler. *Suffering: Human and Divine*. New York: The MacMillan Company, 1939.

Sockman, Ralph W. *The Meaning of Suffering*. New York: Abingdon Press, 1961.

Sontag, Frederick. *God, Why Did You Do That?* Philadelphia: The Westminster Press, 1970.

—*The God of Evil*. New York: Harper & Row, Publishers, 1970.

Sproul, R. C. *Surprised By Suffering*. Wheaton: Tyndale Publishers, Inc., 1988.

Stewart, George. *God and Pain*. New York: George H. Doran Company, 1927.

Taylor, Michael J., editor. *The Mystery of Suffering and Death*. Staten Island, NY: Alba House, 1973.

Tennant, F.R. "The Problem of Evil," *Philosophical Theololgy II*. New York: Cambridge University Press, 1930.

Thomas, George F. *Philosophy and Religious Beliefs*. New York: Charles Scribner's Sons, 1970.

Trout, Virgil. *Christian Evidences*. Austin, Texas: R. B. Sweet Company, Inc., 1963.

Trueblood, Elton. *Philosophy of Religion*. New York: Harper & Row, Publishers, 1957.

Unger, Merrill F. "Satan," *Baker's Dictionary of Theology*. Grand Rapids: Baker Book House, 1973.

Warren, Thomas B. *Have Atheists Proved There Is No God?* Nashville: Gospel Advocate Company, 1972.

Weatherhead, Leslie D. *Salute to a Sufferer*. New York: Abingdon Press, 1962.

—*Why Do Men Suffer?* New York: Abingdon Press, 1936.

Weed, Michael and Willis, Wendell. *Basic Christian Beliefs, Part 2.* Austin, TX: Sweet Publishing Company, 1973.

Wells, Donald A. *God, Man and the Thinker.* New York: Random House, 1962.

Wenham, John W. *The Goodness of God.* Downers Grove, IL: InterVarsity Press, 1974.

Whitcomb, John C., Jr. *The Early Earth.* Grand Rapids: Baker Book House, 1972.

Wiersbe, Warren W. *Why Us? When Bad Things Happen To God's People.* Old Tappan, New Jersey: Fleming H. Revell Company, 1984.

Wright, William Kelly. *A Student's Philosophy of Religion.* New York: The MacMillan Company, 1935.

Yancey, Philip. *Where Is God When It Hurts.* Grand Rapids: Zondervan, 1977.

Yancey, Philip. *Disappointment With God.* Grand Rapids: Zondervan, 1988.

Yandell, Keith E. *Basic Issues in the Philosophy of Religion.* Boston: Allyn & Bacon, Inc., 1971.